The Outsider, V1, No. 1, Fall, 1961

Jon Edgar Webb

Number One

THE OUTSIDER

"Bravo, another
escaping Outsider
. . . enter, man,
and be calmed!"

The OUTSIDER fondly dedicates its No. 1 editorial by fabler Russell Edson to the Academic Quarterlies:

ONE night a horse quit its barn and trotted to the house and put its head through an open window. some humans inside said, look the horse looks inward, in that we who say we are in are looked in on, but for the horse will it not seem that he is looking outward in that he has never seen what we have called *in*.

when they looked again the horse was resting his hindquarters on the windowsill. *look*, the arse of a horse is in the window, taking its ease on the windowsill, that port of inspiration where often we have sought the sunrise.

when they looked again he had shat on the floor below the window. now we are beginning to know something of the horse's mission . . . he came to us knowing that something was again to come into the world, that he was pregnant with an importance needing the cerebral attention of the talking animal . . . that he misinterpreted the natural urge in no way lessens the intention of the beast.

someone said then: surely we should beat the horse's arse out of the window, or bow in prayer to what he left on the floor, or both, just to make sure that in either case we're doing the right thing.

public square

I stepped into the Public Square and looked around. No one noticed me. I looked up. I looked at the spire of the old Terminal Tower. I saw the big clock in the facade of the May Company. I saw a flock of pigeons flying low overhead. I heard many noises —streetcars, automobiles, shuffling feet, newsboys yelling. I kept looking and listening.

I stepped over to the corner of Superior and Ontario Avenues, and stopped in front of the old blind man sitting as I had last seen him.

He was saying, "P. D., Press —Khrushchev, Khrushchev."

"Give me a Press," I said, and gave him a quarter. "Keep the change."

"Thank you."

I looked at his face. Storm-lines streaked it. He had on an old serge suit, a straw hat. He sat on a worn canvas stool.

Suddenly I said, "Mister, what do you see?"

"See? I see nothing," he said. "I'm blind."

"I know," I said. "But what do you see sitting here like this? What do you hear?"

"I see nothing. Khrushchev— I feel nothing — Press? Thank you, lady. See? I only hear."

"What do you hear?"

"Press, Plain Dealer—"

I bent down. "What do you hear?" (*Continued on page 90*)

Sinclair Beiles
Stuart Gordon

metabolic C movies

PALLI WILLI ADULSLA/GUN DI SHTUPI BUM BUM/two lin es of a chant scanned from a spee ded up taperecording of English conversation THE BLOOD WO RD the feedback sucker back wo rd FEED BLOOD sucker back WORD FEED BLOOD BLACK blood feed matter consists of ele ctrically CHARged particles/TER CON LEC CHAR TIC/matter c onsists of ELECTRICALLY CH ARGED PARTICLES/the centr al line being the 'unknown tong ue' (term employed by Shango d ancers of Trinidad "we GONNA HAVE OURSELVES a great big feed--"teach. feed OURSELVES BACK word FEE BLO ORD (S wedish for the devil take YOU word):in SWEDEN the most vicio us form of swearing ROLLS FR OM THE WORD DEVIL the w ord devil THE WORD devil DE HYDRATED FIBRINOGEN th at trantranslates to: ..---, --..-, ..-.. (on or offbeat jazz drummi ng) *all ride-beats to the kick of blood railway* RYE KI TOT BLOO RA Y fibrinogen the clotting agent in the blood; the agent who destroy s kings and princes when he is n ot there argues second time roun d that deal from a laryngeal sna re-drum/LA RINJA LEE DREW

5

MAR/ "well son it's not much o f business with these giant ampli fiers, like insects---get it son---we just let their private blood railw ay tunnel right in. And by.."you ya mean that Dehydrated Fibrin ogen is secretly merged with Priv ate Blood Railroad?.. but I alwa ys dreamed tha ahat Dehydrated Fibrngn was the champ..writhing

ए

.. *say isnt so De. Fibe. Please De. F ib. for all us kids.. say it d. fi.* YO U ARE IN THE WORD AND THE WORD IS IN YOU is a so ng and dance routine/"..Well it 's true I had a little help--"The m usic, the E People.' Yes you my ero take the live blood and sell' t he dead--HARD work it was..'H ARD LIQUID/C ment (sea MC M Metabolic C Movies) THE G REAT WHITE WAIL Metaboli c Sea Metabolic Movies: C.. Met abolic: EPILEPTIC light shutter "met a bolic see.. movies.." TH E GREAT WHITE WAIL by A lbert Einstein (another song and dance routine) : From the quant um phenomena SIPHON THE BLOOD it appears to follow wi th certainty that a finite system o f SLOW DOWN TO ONE FO URTH BEAT finite energy can b e completely described by a finit e set of numbers UNTIL THEY ARE THE MOTHER DRUM (quantum numbers) DRUM TH EY BEAT OUR BLOOD. This d oes not seem to be in accordanc e with a continuum theory. BA RTENDER! ONE BLOOD CE LL MAP TO UNROMANTIC PLACES and must lead to an at

tempt to find a purely algebraic t heory CRISP GRAVITY for the description of reality CRISP GR EENS.. But nobody knows how to obtain CRISP GOODS the b asis of such a GREEN GOODS GRAVITY.. r"3 theory CRISP G NOTES.."Always come due Ital ian Nervi for ONE TWO EINS TEIN tweistein *uno due illusion* R EALITY ILLUSIONI VERITO NI/but no body knows how to o btain a basis for such a theory/P URE ALGEBRA is children lab elled AUTISTIC and catatonic S CHIZOPHRENIA/THE B ritish OFFICER suggests OUT DANC ERS and OUT PHYSICISTS di g the alphabet of TALENTED F LESH IDEOGRAMS confined b y freud in a CERTAIN new jers ey school FOR MENTALLY DI STURBED children MACH OV ER report outioni "TONY" out ony otu to need outonead atton ied AUTO NEED arthhaud kne ed read all about it get your dail y blood: arto *kneed need artoe* ne ed *need our toe/ardo ardo blues* re ad all about it *every word that is written* is absolutely *true*: vampires

ए

: mummifiers: forced fires: churc h spires: griers: cliers: *lost child* n ew jersey clinic *forgot.* . word tre e *sky* found.. out there *woo* O oo o oooossshhh "miss laurry Jane I recon theys a musicalkat n'them nice new nabor folds.." *retreaded charcots tzaras arthauds* argue sec ond time round *the viennese wiza rd* a snare drum with *prison chai ns under* the drumskin! else: 'Th ey gonna do that NICE KNIFE

6

dnae where a body thinks they d one care a body up.. co oming t hrough the 'I' INNER EAR OU TER EAR UBER EAR FREUD NIK pull one out your intestine s Sam E everyone there out surr ea/surrealist retarded entrails alo ne at the glare all night c pauvre typographer c a mis hapen black hoods hanged hoods Podola Gu y Fawkes Gunpowder plots pysc hic nuclear explosion: NO TOM ORROW AND NO 'I' YEAH.. *someone gotta* suck off ya green j uice an we's *cannibals offer* a mu sical suck *better'n steel turn black t o gold..* prince celluloid gypsy se ll you *your flesh like movie low lev el* betrayal ma matador makes it with *every thing once a week* ship t gears fast/GIT LE COUR song

ະຂ

and dance laboratories(approved by institute of good housekeepin g mad ludwig of bavaria medalis t) assure you that FLESH QUA NTA (autistic schizos) can WA VE ROLL OR SWING in new- being ways WIG OR FUNK/to see testimony from fan: "The ho rn in my mouth I blow --nothin g: th then this cat says "rill rr rr ill rrrilll" and I rrrr and out of t hat black cavern out comes a so und *aaa* n and out comes and *so undoundound ounda sounda ssoun da asund asunder asunder saba sa bre* cloven head split j c come wi th sound a sword peace jump ou ta brr brrr brroo burroo braille b raigne cra a a aaa aaaaa aaa aac kkk tablets recom by prof Moshe soo UNDA sounda ssounda ao undda sdo around sounda sasoo

as AOSND asondndsoa *sndodna sdn* THE BEAT IS THE PULSE THE BEAT IN YOU fucks beat ific city NOT JOY MADE the l a/latin quatered the laten QUAR TER/ONE FOURTH BLOOD RATION/one fourth blood beat /Siphon Blood And Sellback deh ydrated fibrogen.. THE BIG BO ARD, pigboard, PBR.. BTI.. so und and SIGHT BLOOD and b e BE EAT, eaten.. WHY NOT?

ະຂ

doug clev testing ein twei dry n s tein: *ali baba rum baba hassan sab a* & thee forty biggest thieves of the lots wife way we like to see u m cowslick"-- and the BEAT W AS THE BE ATE of thee MOT HA DRUM MON" p earl PRIN CE O TRINADADO TRINAM EILINGLO/"Who was that face saw you wi last night Parson Bro wn?"-- "No face that was the wo rd THE WORD.. Theres a story circulatin mongst post nuclear b omb phags/well on my way to th e theatre nobbed cane an spats a n all you never dream what I sa w.. Never? THEIR ANTLERS G REW AN GREW TILL $$ THE Y COULDN get ROUND (of rei ndeer gone extincto tinctured zer o cause thee female arithma antl er standard/case of sexshul relea sers pandled by plas Plasma at la w primordial vendetta.. 'Not blo ody likely guv.. by our lady guv .. by our ole lady GOD SAVE O UR GRACIOUS 666 – the feed back was thee beginning mind.. stuff numerol up your demerol/C an fems argsec tim run tht dl? by personally spikking sellib ate TH

E WORD FEEDBACK flesh qu
anta of n. j. n others YUMYUM
. . the brain needs blood and sug
ar. . ALCHEM CORNERS NE
W BEINGS greenjuice units: I c
optic cupaire per hapsburg. . hae
mophiliacs nourished on greenju
ice jesters/TREND: "Tha lady sa
w you wi las nite--' 'Was no lady,
man --- thas THAT is muh husba
n."/yea suck out the blood & FE
EDBACK THE WORD/new bei
ns fresh with dew BILL BU. . bu
rn burning green fuel DYLAN T
ommy. .PREACHER CAT: (der
saard). . francogerm arab dis hard
. . MAN(faceless)MADE THE W
ORLD *in its image own*/N i john
gold n benita steel of johanannes
burg s. a./basic OWNIMAGE fou
nd in 'The Handbook of Greed'
(the meaning of relatives methue
n sixth edition revisceralise 1956
) Pee 3 compin an feedin steel cr
ystals with pyramids o greenflesh
(travellers' companion green fire
) O fur a leetle bobby cross. . Ho
w abt tradin y chile wi us Billy?. .

℞

corse we charge by the flesh fath
oms/n wherefrum we reach the s
taff, bow-length, lance-length. . th
ereat, with instant skill, the little
Prince pronounced the total of t
he atoms true. . good lord bud k
ept to all his schoolmasters. . doin
wha(a)comes natural or the calcu
lus of the circular *sssssssss*. . His G
ENES SHOT RIGHT OUT FRO
M UNDER HIM/"you can't live
on disseminating tissues forever"
purrs condom . . Pee we 3 can fo
rm new (?) bodies by bringing bo
dies B, C up body A; (obvious ca

se o vampirism)/n say continue t
hen body A such way comes con
tact wi any other body X/the ens
emble of all continuations body
A designate then as space body A
/then's true all bodies r in space o
f the (arbitrarily abour tray rarel
y arbor tray bien seignon arbor t
rays) OKAY everyone YI-YI on t
he SET you virgin springlet rippl
e baby and you there Fire, memb
er baby theez day the day ya lick
Fire out the heaven you gonna S
UCK THE SUN DIG IT MON/
AND WHY NOT? stepping into
musical factory/Took: place--you
groove?--(a) took place in NO JO
Y CITY market-value lobotomy
be's mo precise bout them crack o
doo hush label group probin the
racin stable. . Nah its tetracycline
wi Lulu/Nah could be every jerry
boned built shanty limb from re
OUT/No joyce ity. . the clinic lad
y back after monsoon: you cn go
frig movies you nodamnedgood c
oolie failure the literacy campaig
n/and everyone RECEIVES. . Pic
ture Gall: flesh suckin mon into e
ntire messo life writ by four letta
genies. . cut the plo PLOT Dr. K
nowbelle. . Sure n its Dublin in i
s it?/the God dyin certain sure. . K
een the Googoplex: sying/O they
comin from all ides lord, mouldy
old IDES *ya ta tatat llordy this is a
bourgeois town*. . Y'cn jus see ol d
oc Stanl: *Bring in the ghould*/and a
foot slips under a chicks sweater
like a sailor inna doorway a sno
wy night sullin n lardy nd the do
orwan ans the snowman watchi
n hisself/ILLUSION IS REALIT
Y plus 20 Gnotes/said freudnik pe
nis feeds on paris new jersey USA

8

Gregory Corso

the american way

I am a great American
I am almost nationalistic about it!
I love America like a madness!
But I am afraid to return to America
I'm even afraid to go into the American Express---

II

They are frankensteining Christ in America
   in their Sunday campaigns
They are putting the fear of Christ in America
   under their tents in their Sunday campaigns
They are driving old ladies mad with Christ in America
They are televising the gift of healing and the fear of hell
   in America under their tents in their Sunday campaigns
They are leaving their tents and are bringing their Christ
   to the stadiums of America in their Sunday campaigns
They are asking for a full house an all get out
   for their Christ in the stadiums of America
They are getting them in their Sunday and Wensday campaigns
They are asking them to come forward and fall on their knees
   because they are all guilty and they are coming forward
   in guilt and are falling on their knees weeping their guilt
   begging to be saved O Lord O Lord in their Monday
   Tuesday Wensday Thursday Friday Saturday
   and Sunday campaigns

III

It is a time in which no man is extremely wondrous
It is a time in which rock stupidity
   outsteps danger as the sole enemy in America
It is a time in which ignorance is a good Ameri-cun
Now ignorance is excused only where it is so
   it is not so in America
Man is not guilty Christ is not to be feared

I am telling you the American Way is a hideous monster
    eating Christ   making him into hamburger
    to the taste of its foul mouth
I am telling you the devil is impersonating Christ in America
America's educators & preachers are the mental-dictators
    of false intelligence   they will not allow America to be smart
    they will only allow death to make America smart
Educators & communicators are the lackeys of the American Way
They enslave the minds of the young
    and the young are willing slaves
    because who is to doubt the American Way
    is not the intelligent way?
The duty of these educators is no different
    than the duty of a factory foreman
Replica production   make all the young think alike
    dress alike   believe alike   do alike
Togetherness   this is the American Way
The few great educators in America are weak & helpless
They abide   and so uphold the American Way
Wars have seen such men   they who despised things about them
    but did nothing   and they are the most dangerous
Dangerous because their intelligence is not denied
    and so give faith to the young
    who rightfully believe in their intelligence
Smoke this cigarette doctors smoke this cigarette
    and doctors know
Educators know   but they dare not speak their know
The victory that is man is made sad in this fix
Youth can only know the victory of being born
    all else is stemmed   until death be the final victory
    and a merciful one at that
If America falls it will be the blame of its educators
    preachers   communicators   alike
America today is America's greatest threat
We are old when we are young
America is always new   the world is always new
The meaning of the world is birth not death
Growth gone in the wrong direction
The true direction grows ever young
In this direction what grows grows old
Does the universe grow?   The universe remains
    and thus is ever new
What made earth   a part of the universe
    decide to leave the way of the universe
    and grow another way?

A strange mistake   a strange and sad mistake
    for it has grown into an old thing
    while all else around it is new
Rockets will not make it any younger---
And what made America decide to grow?
I do not know   I can only hold it to the strangeness in man
And America has grown into the American way---
To be young is to be ever purposeful   limitless
To grow is to know limit   purposelessness
Each age is a new age
How outrageous it is that something old and sad
    from the pre-age incorporates each new age---
Do I say the Declaration of Independence is old?
No.   I do say what was good for 1780 is not good for 1960
It was right and new to say all men were created equal
    because it was a light then
But today it is tragic to say it
    sad to even think it
    today it should be fact---
Man has been on earth a long time
One would think with his mania for growth
    he would, by now, have outgrown such things as
    constitutions manifestos codes creeds laws
    that he could well live in the world without them
    and know instinctively how to live and be
    ---for what is being but the facility to love?
Was not that the true goal of growth, love?
Was not that Christ?
But man is strange and grows where he will
    and chalks it all up to Fate   whatever that be---
America rings with such strangeness
It has grown into something strange
    the American is good example of this mad growth
The boy man   big baby meat
    a spoon-fed growth   look to Coca Cola
The American has grown
It was as though the womb were turned backwards
    giving birth to an old child---
The victory that is man does not allow man
    to top off his empirical achievement with death
The Aztecs did it by yanking out the hearts of the young
    at the height of their power
The Americans are doing it by feeding their young to the Way
It was not the Spaniards who killed the Aztec
    it was the Aztec who killed the Aztec

11

Rome is proof   Greece is proof   all history is proof
Victory does not allow degeneracy
It will not be the Communists who will kill America
      no   but America itself---
The American Way   that sad mad process
      is not run by any one man or organization
It is a monster born of itself   existing of its self
The men who are employed by this monster
      are employed unknowingly
They reside in the higher echelons of intelligence
They are the educators the psychiatrists the ministers
      the writers the politicians the communicators
      the religious sects the entertainment world
They are every spokesman of every industry
And some follow and sing the Way because they sincerely
      believe it to be good
And some believe it holy and become missionaries of it
Some are in it simply to be in
And most are in it for gold
Whatever   they do not see the Way as monster
They see it as the "Good Life"
And that because where they arrived they arrived by the Way
And to remain there must uphold the Way
This keeps the Way going---
What is the Way?
The Way was born out of the American Dream
      a nightmare---
The state of Americans today compared to the Americans
      of the 18th century proves the nightmare---
Not Franklin not Jefferson who speaks for America today
      but strange red-necked men of industry
      and the goofs of show business
Bizzare!   Frightening!   The court jester sits on the throne
      and Hollywood has a vast supply---
Could grammar school youth seriously look upon
      a picture of George Washington and Herman Borst
      the famous night club comedian by his side at Valley Forge?
Old old and decadent   gone the dignity
      the American sun seems headed for the grave
O that youth could raise it anew!
The future depends solely on the young
The future is the property of the young
What the young know the future will know
What they are and do the future will be and do
What has been done must not be done again

Will the American Way allow this?
No.
I see in every American Express
        and in every army center in Europe
        I see the same face   the same sound of voices
        the same clothes_ the same walk .
And beside them I see their mothers & fathers
        there is no difference among them
        but that they are young and their parents old---
Replicas
Indeed the Way has given birth to 170 million-tuplets---
They not only speak and walk and think alike
        they have the same face!
What did this monstrous thing?
What regiments a people with similar tastes?
How strange is nature's play on America
        ---for what is it that makes them *look* alike?
Surely were Lincoln alive today
        he could never be voted President   not with his looks---
Indeed Americans are babies all in the embrace
        of Mama Way
Did not Ike, when he visited the American Embassy in Paris
        a year ago, say to the staff---"Everything is fine,
        just drink Coca Cola, and everything will be all right."
This is true, and is on record.
Did not American advertising call for TOGETHERNESS?
        This is true, and is on record.
Are not the army centers in Europe ghettos?
        They are, and O how sad   how lost!
The PX newsstands are filled with comic books!
The army movies are always Doris Day and Rock Hudson!
They have brought the American Way to Europe
        and they keep it in the areas allotted them
        filling it with recreation centers and ladies clubs
        when all around them is opera museums cities to behold
        but they never leave their ghetto
        look to Harlem and see America in Berlin
What makes a people huddle so?
Why can't they be universal?
Who has smalled them so?
This is serious! I do not mock or hate this
        I can only sense some mad vast conspiracy!
Helplessness is all it is!
They are caught   caught in the Way---
And those who seek to get out of the Way

do not
The Beats are good example of this
They forsake the Way's habits
        and acquire for themselves their own habits
And they become as distinct and regimented and lost
        as the main flow
        because the Way has many outlets
        like a snake of many tentacles—
There is no getting out of the Way
The only way out is the death of the Way
And what will kill the Way but a new consciousness
Something great and new and wonderful must happen
        to free man from this beast
It is a beast we can not see or even understand
It is the condition of our minds
God how close to science fiction it all seems!
As if some power from another planet
        incorporated itself in the minds of us all
It could well be!
For as I live I swear America does not seem like America to me

Americans are a great people
        and they believe in those in whom they entrust power
And those who have the power are a great people
        and they are endeared to the people who have entrusted them
Fine—
But what strangeness has made the men of power
        and the people under that power
        become one and alike—the same being?
I ask for some great and wondrous event
        that will free us from the Way
        and make us a glorious purposeful people once again
I do not know if that event is due   deserved
        or even possible—
I can only hold that man is the victory of life
And I hold firm to American man

I see standing on the skin of the Way
        America   as proud and victorious as St. Michael
        on the neck of the fallen Lucifer—

Jon Edgar Webb, Jr.

a peek over the wall

Slowly going up against the grain and bastards who sit behind desks and tell dirty jokes in the men's room—severing the rope that held so tight so long since the birth just to rise up above heads and peek . . . and all is clear and you smile at your fears: the time you two went into each other with a line tied to soul juices, tearing at volition and shifting position to a beat lost with a thud of bursting hearts long quelled by inhibition, but now laugh like a funeral fly . . . depth and conception distorting shape and matter swollen in the rain of time, lost in the grass on Saturday night, regained on Sunday and held like a letter to lick hot with lipstick and syrupy perfume and sent to the person who stood next you and pressed a bony hip against yours, while you moved away hoping it would follow, and remembered at bedtime down under the sheets with playing hands like children glued to a cat's fleabitten tail, but never decided completely the best way, for you dreamed of the person that didn't wear underwear and never went to the toilet or smelled of perspiration nor made black rings on the bathtub or smudged kleenex in the park . . . no not like the others who owned dirty rectums and brushed their murky cigarette-stained teeth, singing hymns in their fat hairy nude with ingrown toenails and piles; so you waited until time boiled and erupted and virginity smelled awful and hair touched in the dark was hot and wet and hell was your sister, or brother, and food tasted like dirt under an elephant at full term pregnancy, and your thighs rode over each other and were moist and the bitchy bastards,

15

all, were just like your teacher, and the others . . . so you ran to the
other side of correctness and threw your identity over the spider's web
and spread open your intellect and thirst for consciousness and one-
ness and earth-rock and cinnamon kisses and tingling breasts no
matter to hell the day the door might open and God would shout
through his whiskers. That's why you refused any other answer because the splinter was of bone sliced privately and where it wouldn't
show no matter whose hand you kissed or lips kissed yours. You can
yell now to hell with yesterday's neatly folded underwear and the
hung ankle suit and the guest's pink toiletpaper can go out the window with the keyhole that showed humanity and down under, and
you're right now in your madness to grasp the sweet touch of deeper
than skin hormones and laughter that stills the stinking space of universe into which you never had any good excuse to enter; and forget
forever mother in her giant wedding rings who always smiled when
she said bastard to father who never smiled when he said anything
or brother who rode the light bulbs out of the house and stole sister's
puberty panties and locked himself in the bathroom and plugged up
the keyhole, and sister who stole mother's pads before she needed
them and ran around with tom podney on his handlebars licking pop-
sicles, showing the boys behind nick's bar her titties and who knows;
and dad's relation who tried to with you in the back seat but cut a
hand on the broken window when you hollered and because you were
too young not to. But worse was the life than the promises to come,
like the time in the water and the fish began nibbling and you stay-
ed until the sun went down, laughing—but now so many years later
you suddenly see over the wall . . . so scream and scram to reality,
now you see the use of born flesh and brain not to be wasted toying
with blind eyeballs and fluttering lashes or children with snot running
down purple cheeks or diaper pins poked in the wallpaper or the hard
dried gum stuck under the table or stale jokes; now you know truth
and God in his whiskers knows too and doesn't mind you knowing and sits too far off to smell like the cod dad hooked and didn't
bring home till after he caught syphillis and knocked your two front
teeth out. Damn, you see the truth now and can't wait to rake your
rear over the ice and cool leaves of the darker part of the woods so
that the long wet hot grass is no longer impersonal and feels wonderful and uninhibited, and you can laugh like an idiot now when one
who wishes to be THE one writes

Youar drawkcab
all th time
you look drawkcab
at yer past
passed
Backward Angel

kiss m yass
I paid the rint and
got yer beer
loved ya sweety
thanked God for ya
but ya drawkcab as ole
ya got my soul
Youar drawkcab . . .

laugh and pull at the string that is tied to heaven and truth and self-
identity and (for better or for worse) honey straight from the bee.

Ann Giudici

three poems

Be careful when you step toward me with
heavy feet,
eager to prove your manhood
and me the cost.

This has been too long building
and the value of my soft, white steel flesh
makes you easy to kill.

No tiger in the trees,
my feet are light and the soles soft and easy
and will come with care from under
to take from you the offending,
witless parts.

I was a child and didn't know who loved me.
Offering soft violence so they would look;
splashes of dance through the heavy rooms,
floors scratched by my grasping feet;

peep shows dug in the ground to see the fairies.

Mama, Mama, look at me; I'm flying.
Mama, Mama, look; it's bleeding.

Running through long halls to escape the
lumbering bear;
into a room, raising the flat faces.

Mama, Mama, I'm gone now.

I grew from the end of the hall, down the stairs,
out into the streets.
I found other children looking,
I found that fairies live in peep shows
and are approachable, Mama, if you smile.

Mama, Mama, I'm gone now.
Did you know that?

🙠

Can you pause and stay with me,
warm, lovely boy
with the earth singing,
moving hugely at your direction.
The beginning of sight,
love already on you;
rising passion held close, secretly,
warming me.

Your pleasure leaps over reason,
falls, recovers,
laughing pulls back.

Shall I wait for youth to catch me,
hang worriedly to hard flesh,
sit calm, placid and watch errors,
knowing better ways;
or tear away, knowing this day would if could
at least be mine.

lord jim

forcing it thru yr teeth like the red syrup
that keeps us from coughing at night
I have begun to walk toward it,
                    it is very beautiful
                    I shall walk toward it
all my flesh
protesting, do you see, the sun makes light
by exploding, by eating away

I am not afraid.   That is a lie
                    & it is another lie
to say I will stay.

I SHALL WALK TOWARD IT
                    the green ice flickers & leaps
the summer shall send down hail
I want very little:

that you shd make light/make love
                    consent
to be corroded, blind, the hissing steam
rising at once from both of us

In the summer the empty lot, at the end of the sidewalk
is covered w/matted grasses, dry, the flickering
backs of beetles . . .

thru the uncertainty, the poise
                    of listening.
The drop of ink falls.   It lands.   It makes a shape.
SOMEONE HAS CRIED OUT TO ME, HAS ASKED FOR LIFE
something has stirred in there, behind the trees.
I am afraid of the shapes I must make on the stage
all the air I must cut thru.

I am afraid of yr face, yr silence, the laught
w/which you carry it off.
I want to tell you we'll die
                    why stand for it
why take what's offered, why not walk out toward
the green & flickering sea that comes to meet us

19

John Grant

"Look, Ma—No Hands!"

on the dot

"Want one of these . . . . ?

"What are they"

"Full-stops. Try one. They're good." .

"   .   Thanks—what do I do with it"

"Put it at the end of sentences. Like this. Look I'll do it again. See the difference? Now say something."

"I don't know what to say"

"That'll do. Now put a full-stop at the end of it."

"I don't know what to say. I get it. This is great! Give me another one."

"Here. Catch. Here's some more . . . . . . You'll need these too , , , , , , , ? ? ? ? ? ? ? ? They'll help you until you get on your feet. Nobody gets through life without full-stops and a few question marks."

"Say, these punctuation marks are great little things. Things are going to be a lot easier from now on. Thanks."

"It's nothing. There's plenty more where they came from. I just wanted to help you out so we could have ourselves a little talk. Can't talk without the equipment."

"What d'you want to talk about?"

"Anything you say."

"I don't know what to say"

"The last time you said that I told you to put a full-stop after it."

"I don't know what to say. Unless I tell you about the nun."

"A *nun?*"

20

"Nun. I saw a nun today and you know what she was doing?"

"What?"

"*Buying* funny postcards. A *nun*."

"Maybe she was on holiday."

"I don't know. Nuns don't go on holiday do they? Do nuns go on holiday?"

"I don't know. Suppose they must same as everybody else. Got yours fixed yet?"

"What? Got *what* fixed?"

"Your holidays."

"My *holidays*. Yes. All fixed up. Going to Italy this year. I'll send you a funny postcard. Maybe I'll see her there."

"See who?"

"The *nun*. That's where most of them are isn't it! In Italy? I wonder who she'd be sending a postcard to."

"Another nun I suppose."

"Do you think so? A funny postcard to a *nun*?"

"She could write in Latin on the back. Did I ever tell you about the postcard I got once?"

"No."

"Well I got this postcard from a minister and he wrote a little prayer on the back."

"A funny one?"

"No. One of these *holy* prayers all about—"

"I mean a funny *postcard*."

"No. It was a coloured one. A view. One of these coloured ones with a view. But *still*—on a *postcard*, for God's sake."

"You got yours fixed?"

"What?"

"*Your* holidays."

"Me? No, I don't know what to do this year. I had thought about Russia. I've always wanted to go to Russia."

"You won't see any funny postcards *there*."

"I won't see any *nuns* either."

"You know, I didn't mean she was buying *sexy* postcards. They were just these funny ones."

"I know, I know. I didn't think she'd buy *sexy* ones."

"You got a girl-friend? I don't mean to get personal or anything but—"

"No. I used to though."

"I hope you don't think I'm being—"

"It's okay. Just those sexy postcards made you think about it. It's okay."

"I suppose they did. It's funny how people get *ideas* don't you think."

"Yes I think sometimes."

"I mean don't you think it's funny how people get ideas and keep *saying* things all the time? *Talking* I mean. Like us."

"Suppose it is come to think of it. Where did you say you saw this nun?"

"In that shop next the post office. She was just going *into* the post office last I saw."

"And was she, I mean did she look embarrassed?"

"No. She didn't look embarrassed. She was just white-looking. You know—*pale.*"

"Maybe she was worrying in case somebody saw her. Maybe that's why she was pale."

"All nuns are white like that. At least all the ones I've seen have been *very* white. She was just going into the post office to get stamps for her postcards. How much do you think it would cost to send a postcard from Italy? Have you any idea?"

"I don't know. You afraid it's going to cost too much? I think you get cheap-rate if you write a prayer on the back."

"Did that minister *really* send you a postcard with a prayer on the back?"

"Sure he did. He really did. You just reminded me when you talked about that nun."

"I saw a picture about a nun once. She fell in love with this soldier, only she wouldn't tell him because she was a *nun.*"

"What'd she do? Send him a postcard?"

"She just prayed and prayed until it passed. Cigarette?"

"Thanks."

"Have *you* ever noticed how everybody says 'thanks' all the time. Sometimes I'm sitting in a bus and I listen to the conductor and he keeps saying 'thanks' and 'thank you.' *All* the time. And the people getting tickets they say 'thanks' too. Everybody does."

"What's wrong with that?"

"Nothing. Nothing's wrong with that. But it just seems funny that they should keep saying 'thanks' like that *all* the time when they don't even *mean* it."

"They've got to say something."

"Yes, that's it. I mean it's funny how you get ideas and just *say* things all the time. You even say things you don't mean. You ever do that?"

"Sure. Everybody does. Everybody says things they don't mean."

"I mean just talking like this. I like it. It's got full-stops and everything. But it just seems so pointless sometimes. Talking all the time I mean. To people."

"Sure it does. That's why Mendelssohn wrote songs without words."

"Why did Mendelssohn write songs without words?"

"Because it was pointless."

"You mean he didn't use full-stops like us?"

22

"Sure he did. He just didn't use *words*, that's all. Want to hear my favourite one?"

"Please."

"Let's see—hm—I'm not much of a singer but here goes.

                '   ,   ?

                        ,   .

                        !   ?   ;

                ;   ;   .

                ,   :

                    ,

                !   .   ,

                !   ,   !

                                                ?

                ,   !

                                    ;

                    ?   .'

Did you like that?"

"Just about the nicest thing I've ever heard. And in German too. I didn't know you could sing in German. Is that it all? Is that the whole thing?"

"No. There's a second verse but I've forgotten the punctuation."

"Where are you going?"

"I've run out of full-stops and commas Coming with me to that shop next to the post office? They sell them there Flavoured ones"

"Sure thing. Maybe I can show you that nun if she's still there. Here, have one of mine.   ."

Paul Haines

. . . had spent laughing

now can YOU imagine that hyper-hip SF Set,
run into twisting Dickens & coming up
with one good word for DICK,

learning who Wilde got busted on in 307,
Savoy Hotel, was Charles Parker; can you
imag---or maybe, f'd anyway, laugh . . .

23

Gary Snyder

xrist

Your hanging face I know, I know your tree.
You can't hide under Hebrew
              & I don't pity you
Burning yrself alive in Athens to impress the mob
Having your last wild fling (in drag) at the altar—
             robed in cornstarch
              & stolen Toltec jewels
                      Ziggurat rotgut
Cutting your own balls off—dog priests—Cybele
The mincing step—shy glance—(Graves thought you
                       lame)
Horrified virgin dropping in a pool.

                  Whipping the bullshit roarer
Your flayed penis flaring
Gold wrought infibula
            —circumcized girls.

New World popcorn, Polynesian spit—
Dropping a log on the couple where they fuck
                the dance, the whips
Saviour of Man!
           —who put the hell to be harrowed?

The bruised snake coils in the grass
He is wise;
             there are trees in high places;
Keep your blood off the crotch of our tree.

Gael Turnbull

a hill

Black upon orange, a profile of giant rubble, for a moment it
barricades the sun. Orange out of black, a foliage of wrinkled
copper, for a moment dawn germinates in a furrow of the hill.

The phrases are apt. The scene is not unusual. The joy is in
the attention.

The description is not a circumscribed likeness; that is, of any
delimited hill. It is not that, nor is it exactly at random.

The description portrays a hill which is discovered in the action;
an unknown hill which becomes known, which is a likeness,
and which becomes likely.

It is Bredon Hill. It is a name. But it is not that.

It is a whale, dark indigo, partly submerged, the dorsum crusted
with shell-fish. And it is not.

It is asleep, folded upon itself, eyelids and mouth sunk into
forehead and cheek, an old man taking a nap. And it is not.

It is awake, a heraldic beast, crouched, to stare westward, alert
for the Malverns, its eyes fixed upon Clee Hill and the Long
Mynd, its nostrils dilated to sense far beyond into the hills
of Wales. And it is not.

It is archeologists from Birmingham, bearded students and tweedy
spinsters, digging in the earthworks near Overbury, excited by
old bones, pottery fragments, tabulating, speculating, defining
pit dwellings in the chalk. And it is not.

It is a young couple who have modernised an old cottage at Great
Comberton, with a Van Gogh print in the living room, and a
three year old Morris Minor in the garage. And it is not.

It is the damp, dew dripping through the bracken, oozing slick
upon clay and flint, soaking down into the meadows, and
delicately settling in microscopic drops on the backs of

25

the sheep between the twisted filaments of wool. And it is not.

It is an afternoon yet to come, a picnic with sandwiches and cider,
the children riding happy on the turf, with bees in the gorse,
and a slight sunburn. And it is not.

And it is. The description is made. The attention becomes explicit.
The hill has become familiar.

It has become a description, not a hill. But it declares a hill, a
very particular hill, a remarkable hill: a hill which it is
possible to know.

Charles Olson

Borne down by the inability to lift the heaviness,
        and Zeus walks off with Ganymede smiling

My eyes down cast while talking at too much distance
from my friend,
        and Zeus walks on, and off with Ganymede

The days all the fall of the year and man and woman calling
for a new deal,

      and there Zeus is with his fillet tilted and the tilt
      in his eye,

      and he comes right through, snatching
      the boy as he goes

How light I am if I thought of it and hot
if I were inside one foot distance

      And the boy lets him, gaily
      with a lock falling on his captor's shoulder

      and still holding the cock he had, Ganymede
      lets Zeus walk off with him, smiling

like a message on sunday

Sits

the forlorn plumber

by the river

with his daughter
staring at the water
then, at her

his daughter, closely.

Once, world,
he came
to fix the stove,
and couldn't
oh, we were impatient, doesn't
a man know what he is doing?

We were impatient,
the man couldn't,
His occupation
is his occupation, world of iron thorns

sitting by his daughter
by the water

I stare into that plumber
so that I can see a daughter in the water
she thin and silent.
He, wearing a baseball cap

in a celebrating town this summer season
may they live on

on, may their failure be kindly, and come
in small pieces.

Allen Ginsberg

the end

(to KADDISH)

God answers with my doom! I am annulled, this poetry blanked
    from the fiery ledger,
my lies be answered by the worm at my ear, visions by the beard
    that covers my trembling jaw like monster-skin,
longing to be God by my hand falling over my eyes to cover them
    from sight of the skeleton
My stomach vomiting out the soul-vine, nightmare rising out of my
    blood on mortal floor in bamboo hut, body-meat crawling
    to its fate,
The noise of the drone of creation adoring its slayer, the yowp of
    birds to the infinite,
dogbarks like the sound of vomit in the air, frogs croaking death
    at trees,
I am a Seraph and I know not whither I go in the Void, I am a man
    and I don't know whither I go into death—
Christ Christ poor hopeless lifted on the Cross between dimensions
    —to enter the ever-Unknowable
A mad gong shivers thru all flesh and the vast Being enters my brain
    from afar that lives forever
None but the Presence too mighty to record! the presence in Death!
    before whom I am helpless,
Makes me change from Allen to a skull — Old OneEye of dreams
    in which I do not wake but die—
hands pulled into the Darkness by a frightful Hand —-the worm's
    blind wriggle, cut — the plough is God Himself,
What ball of monster darkness before the universe come back to
    visit me again with blind Command!
and I can blank out this consciousness, escape back to New York
    love,
and will, poor pitiable Christ afraid of the foretold cross, never
    to die,
escape but not forever, — the Presence will come, a strange truth
    enter my life again,
Death show its Being as before and I'll despair that I *forgot! forgot!*
    to take it back, tho die of it.

What's sacred when the Thing is all the universe? Creeps to every
    soul like a vampire organ singing in the bearded stars—
I'll die in horror that I die — if I forget — and this is no illusion.
Not dams or pyramids but death, and we to prepare for that
    nakedness,
poor bones sucked dry by His long mouth of ants and wind, & our
    souls murdered to prepare his Perfection—
The moment's come, He's made his will revealed forever — and no
    flight into old Being
further than the stars will not find terminal in the same dark swaying
    port of unbearable music,
No refuge in Myself on fire, or in the world which is His also to bomb
    & devour—
Recognise His might! Loose hold of my hands! my frightened skull
    — for I had chose self-love,
my nose, my cock, my face, my soul — and now the faceless
    Destroyer—
A billion doors to the same new Being! the universe turns inside out
    to devour me—
poor being come squat in a dark field in Peru to drop my load —
    When the mighty burst of music comes from out the inhuman
    Door.

Peru, 1960

Peter Orlovsky

snale poem

Make my grave shape of heart so like a flower be free aired & hand-
    some felt.
Grave root pillow, tung up from the grave & wigle at blown up clowd.
Ear turnes close to underlayer of green felt moss & sound of rain
    drible thru
    this thin layer down to the roots that will tickle my ear.
Hay grave, my toes need cutting so file away in soung curve. or
Garbage grave, way above my head, blood will soon trickle into my
    ear—
    no choise but the grave so cat & sheep are daisey turned.
Train will tug my grave, my breath hueing gentil vapor between weel
    & track.
So kitten string & ball, jumpe over this mound so gently & cuteyly
    so my toe can curl & become a snale & go cureosity on its way.

29

doorknobs

The simple silly terror
of a doorknob on a door
that turns to let in life
on two feet standing,
walking, talking,
wearing dress or trousers,
maybe drunk or maybe sober,
maybe smiling, laughing, happy,
maybe tangled in the terror
of a yesterday past grandpa
when the door from out there opened
into here where I, antenna,
recipient of your coming,
received the talking image
of the simple silly terror
of a door that opens
at the turning of a knob
to let in life
walking, talking, standing
wearing dress or trousers,
drunk or maybe sober,
smiling, laughing, happy,
or tangled in the terror
of a yesterday past grandpa
not of our own doing.

Juan Martinez

work song

I wake up with the cover fights, all twisted in the sheet and
struggling like always after too much to drink the night before.
The dull ache, and the goddam alarm ringing—electric, what kind
of man would make an electric alarm? I push the button with one
hand, and with the nice easy swinging motion—even with the
dull ache that good—I wave my fingers and the room comes into
place with me at the center of it, then Maria, and the bed, the
broken up floorboards all gouged from the cheap metal furniture
that Maria buys from which the plastic tips come off bumpbump
all around the room, scraping up the floorvarnish, and then
thump thump noises on the ceiling below where the Shumakers let
us know they hear that noise again. Then the walls, all white,
nice white, clean, done by me with white paint that comes in sacks
for only 30 cents a lb. which makes the space clean, then the
enamel copper virgin on the wall—Maria's because she is living in
sin she tells me—and the paintings.

The sun is on the wall now, and I see that I used too much
what Gregory who made it to the Fine Arts with his GI bill money
calls "high intensity," (smart cat that Gregory...). But this is
all right. The painting makes it anyway, even with the sun and
the dull ache—this is because my mind is ordered with clean space,
and Maria being alright, and not bugged by her folks, who are
very religious and get her all screwed up with wondering. This
makes me feel good, and I say Ha, Gregory, you don't know so
damn much, damn you.

With which saying Maria shuffles the covers, and I pull the
sheet down from her creamy brown spick-and-spade shoulders
(which is a local joke, like they say, because Maria's mother is a
spik and her father is a spade) and the little muscles ripple on the
back, and her arms curl around her shoulders to keep warm, with
long fingers caressing herself in love along the back. Oh Maria!
Warm rounds of curves along the shoulders, and then stretched-
muscle back tapering down to little waist, and (pulling back more
covers), hot heaps of buttocks tense as passion even in sleep.
I take my thumb and run it down her spine into the warm crack.

31

Maria grunts and pushes it away. I do it again. "God*damn* it Johnny!" she says, "don't you nevah get enough?" I laugh and jump from the bed *wham* both feet on the cold floor, because now I know she wants it, and I'll wait now until tonight which will be even better. Oh Maria!

Now swoosh into the bathroom, swinging on this white space and the paintings and even Maria's copper virgin. Buzz with the old electric shaver—Maria's present which Gregory says is a bad thing and an example of how they're fucking us with all these things to buy, but which I use anyway because quicker. Ohla, vududuh reep-AH . . . still swinging, the dull ache almost gone now, sunlight coming through the white curtain, big and gold on the wall. Now out to the kitchen, pop with the icebox door, grab chow (mexican breakfast my ass), and hit the wine, swinging swinging out past Maria who with one dark eye peering sideways out from the white sheet all mingled with thick nightropes of spick-and-spade hair gives me the look—got her now boy, I say to myself, smiling at her with those curves of shoulders waiting, the full line down to the tits swelling up over the sheet.

Slam! the door (hell with the Shumakers who sleep too much anyway, all tired out from bitching), and blam blam down the stairs, only hitting twice from landing to landing, banking like a race driver, with one hand holding onto the posts as I swing past the corners, down from the roof-floor to the street, giving one glance back at the skylight under which is Maria still stretching, and bang, perfect timing past three suits and a secretary onto the Broadway bus.

Nothing happens now for an hour. Drowze, drowze, bus fumes, jingle in the coin box, drowze . . . nothing.

I give em the badge with one hand at the gate (thank you, fuckyaverymuch) and go out on the pier to the job. Foghorns still blow Varuumph, Vaaaruuumph out in the sound, a little low fog down her still. But not much, just a little and thinning. The bruised boards on the pier still this dark mystic not-purple, not-brown, which I haven't got figured out yet, but which I will any day now—got to stop thinking about which color I *think* it is so the old eyes can *see* . . . it was the same way with the water with fog on it for a long time, but which I've got now up on the roof-floor all white in the sun . . .

"Okay Martinez—" says Anderson. Dumb swede of a foreman, five minutes before the whistle blows he starts. If I were a dumb swede like him I'd get the union on him—but no, I tell him I *like* to start early. "Hell," I say, "sooner we start, sooner we get done, hey?" Which gets him worse than having the union on him, because it ruins his screw-up for him. Hah!

32

He takes me over by the shed where they have the new barrels and gives me a bunch of wind about being sure to wipe off the bungs before I open em up. Which I know anyway, but which takes up time so that when the whistle blows nobody can say his crew was working before seven.

Okay, so now we start. Slow easy rhythms, not getting worked up about it, I open twenty or thirty bungs and stick the chrome rod into the first one. Then I pick up one of the little rags from the box, hold the rod over a test can, wipe the oil off, screw the top back on and mark it: September 17, 1960, Lot 2237, #2957482J. The J gets em—big executive.

I keep doing this until the sun is up level with the shed roof and the dock has this steam coming off it, drying up. Inside the shed now I can hear the forklift going, skidding back and forth, Malloy gunning it all the while, giving it hell, all pissed off at that damn fork truck, going to make foreman before he's thirty. . . . Oof! I hear him drop a' pallet. This is what Gregory means. Me, I just take it easy now, checking one barrel of fishoil at a time, making very sure to wipe those bungholes like the man says. Cause I know he's back there with the agent having himself a game of checkers before he figures he'll pop out here just before noon to catch me washing up early. Yassir, I'm just a dumb mex, won't make foreman by the time I'm a hundred and sixty-seven years old anyway, don't have that old get up and get it right in the ass bounce like old Mrs. Malloy in there cussing over his forklift.

Now comes Anderson with the sad-and-means written all over, just can't beat that goddamn agent, then comes the whistle and I tighten up that bung I've been fooling with for the last ten minutes and make it to the washtrough. "Jesus," Malloy says, "I dint think lunch'ud ever come! You oughta feel the heat build up in that shed." Yeah, yeah.

Now out past the gate that says YOU ARE NOW LEAVING HARBOR ISLAND, like Welcome to Woodenville, pop. 312., all good-natured for the tourists getting the old eyeballs washed out with local color, and then across the street against the light, and into the diner. "Well, well," says old Alice with the big winter-comforter ass, "look who we got here—first as usual."

I give her the line back, and she says, "Hey I heard you sold some pitchers the other day," so I come on modest of course cause I know I can afford to, it being in Frank Lynch's column in the Post-Intelligencer that one Juan Martinez, which is me, is thought to be doing all right, and that he is having this show, and all that. So that no matter what I say I will look good. This makes me hungry as hell, and I feel a little jumped up like I used to before I got everything straightened away inside me, orderly with space for the

33

mind to paint, so I have another beer and get the sads a little. Thinking about everything, painting troubles, and Maria's folks, and how Gregory who I have known all this while, kids together right down off Jackson Street (ex-slum kid, Frank Lynch says),— how Gregory isn't making it, painting or lifewise, like they say, because he is all hung up on all these things that are happening to everybody, me and him and the whole world right from the Pike Place Market up to Washington D. C. So I have another beer.

"Jesus," Alice says, wiping at the cigarette burns on the counter but looking at me sucking up that beer—"Jesus, you going to work or not?"

"Oh Alice, pretty Alice," I say, making her feel good—a real killer with the women—"lets you and me just run away together to some desert island and never come back. How about that, Alice?"

"Huh!" she says, still working at those cigarette burns. So I leave her a buck, which means a 15-cent tip—15 cents more than she gets from anyone else today—then I hop on out of there, and make it back in time to have a cigarette while I look at the sun blasting away at Puget Sound, building up all that heat for Mrs. Malloy inside the shed.

The afternoon goes fast. I run out of barrels about three o'clock, everybody in the country can have their vitamins now, all that fishoil labelled, ready for testing. So I mess around wiping off the bungs, doing a good job again, and pretty soon the whistle blows and I'm on my way out of there. As I make it around the corner I see old Malloy looking saggy, fishing a cigarette out of his denim shirt with a weary look, all stiff like an enamelled virgin. Then I'm gone.

In the bus again. Lots of newspapers, all folded, everybody finding out what the sexkiller did to Mary Jane. Then I think about Lynch's column again, and I feel good, so I stop off at Stangl's place on the way home. This cat is very weird, and paints a little like Morris Graves, who is from Seattle, and who also paints like hell. We talk for awhile, passing the shit back and forth, and I sneak a look at what he's got on the easel, only I don't say anything. Then it begins to hit me because it is very strong stuff, lots of stems in it, and I get the dull ache again.

Jesus, I think of Maria. Okay Jack, I say, it's sure been nice making it with you and all that jazz, and pop blam, I'm on the street again, and making it home. Oh me the sun is already making it down between the houses, darkspace, and then flash, dark space and then flash as I hit an open space—nice rhythms which I feel and which I will put down when I get home as soon as I hit the sack with Maria. The sidewalk feels tilted, I am always walking down hill, going easy, everything making it, got the giggles a little—

the sun, and the houses needing paint, and the neon lights
beginning to show where the hills are in shadow. Goddamn,
Johnny Martinez, I think with all this going on inside me, you are
one lucky fucker.

   With this I look up and see the light coming out of the skylight, with old sexy Maria under it, probably panting her ass off,
and I swing in through the doors, and start climbing the stairs,
asking myself whether it's going to be before chow or afterward, but
knowing damn well it is going to be before, and already feeling
how it's going to be *good*.

Gilbert Sorrentino

ave atque vale

We are going away now,
goodbye, goodbye, we are
slowly leaving you, we
are disappearing in eddies

of smoke, the trees are
around us, and I know
you thought we would stay
but we are moving away

now, more swiftly, it
seems. We. Who moved
nowhere for so long, that
is a strange animation

there? It is I and
you, dear, we are leaving
ourselves now slowly, see
our friends speaking to us

as we depart an inch
or two above the grass, I
can just see you there and I
beside you, goodbye.

35

Walter Lowenfels

good-bye jargon

Elegy for a small press

Since 1492 some 172 million of us in the U.S.A. have
    advanced from deserts, wastes, forests and lonesome prairie
to a thruway of cities, highways and missile bases with
    unemployed men and women on every corner.
There is still one practically uninhabited mountain pass
    and that's the poetry-crossing over Big Muddy.
Publish a book of poems in the Strontium Age and you can enjoy
    all the rigors of striking out on a new Oregon Trail.
The rapids, the natives, the rain, the heat, the cold, the thunder
    —they're all there—particularly the long lonesome days and
    nights when you don't see a chipmunk reader peering
    across the poetry route along the Columbia River highway of
    our dreams.

When you consider there are 400,000 of us turning out the stuff
    these days and several hundred of us proclaimed the "Greatest
    Poets of our Generation," you can realize what a huge vacuum
    our non-readers are creating.
Do you wonder the earth is slipping on her axis and the moon is
    a decimal off-center every other thousand years?
    There aren't enough poetry readers turning pages
    to keep the side-slip of our jet travel around the
    universe on an even keel.
We are slipping down the hydrogen side of the galactic spiral

with poems receding from our unreading eyes and
everybody wonders can the next explosion save us from
smashing our lovely planet without even an elegy for
its good-bye.
In the great silence even Tiberius no longer asks "what song
the sirens sang" because what the Emperor of Today hears
is the mushroom screaming.
And that's the song.

welcome home to cubby

Among 16,000 insane inmates he was the conscious maniac.
He doesn't want to be "normal." He can't stand the
sexless odor of it.
Something happened to him—in the navy—in the army—
in the Red Hook dives of his Brooklyn underworld. The lining
of his country's stomach got turned inside
out for him and he saw what he couldn't
swallow.
Some people say he's nothing but a dirty writer.
I hear the pinprick of what he has lost dropping
its specimen over the Flatbush Avenue marshes.
Of course we can't stand it. It's our personal fall-out
trickling down the Gulf Stream. It's the crotch
of our Pentagon's cleanest H-bomb. It's the other
self we are trying to turn our backs on—the corpse
of the old Dog-Eat-Dog lousing up Rockefeller
Plaza years after it should have been laid out.
It's too late now for burial. It has to be cremated.
Meanwhile, to participate in the ceremony, Cubby
himself has to burn.
That hiccough laugh he gives as he talks and grabs for his
anti-allergy pills hasn't to do with anything funny.
He's allergic to the universe. He's looking for
everlasting love in the urinals. It's the acid drop
of human intercourse that is biting him. He is
working toward that one word that will drop us all without an
echo of his being alive alongside three billion others for whom
his desperation is the tombstone they have to overturn
if they are to survive.

37

Cid Corman

two poems

POST MORTEM

I shall be dead a long time.
I expect that. And the quiet
slow. As if there were
nothing but quiet.

No sky. Of course, no sky.
I didn't expect it. Nothing
surprising. No face
to crowd into the heart.

No heart. No heaviness.
Absence will be thorough.
I wont know it. Earth
has no time to remember me.

No time. And no desire.
And no sound of wings,
of a breeze. No breath.
I shall not be dead any longer.

SEMPRE D'AMORE

Bruno, you and I and Elvi again,
and just to say it exceeds desire, plays
as the night-lightning did, breaking lashed rain,
about my heart, lifting the darkness in ...

There we drank confusion, muttered love, stared.
A black sycamore guarding the front door
says, Stay, stay. And we stay, as if stained deeper
by something we cannot, dare not, say. Say,

Why should we fear and yet we fear: as if
the rocks that we walk down to see in the Piave,
white in themselves, washed whiter by the stream,
smoothed and rounded, sounded a depth in us.

We stopped then and we stop now; I stop.
Where you and I and Elvi picked a flower,
a wild scarlet on a weak spindle, a color
stands. I stand and for us mark a place,
                              a passage.

underwear

I didn't get much sleep last night
thinking about underwear
Have you ever stopped to consider
underwear in the abstract
When you really dig into it
some shocking problems are raised
Underwear is something

we all have to deal with
Everyone wears
some kind of underwear
Even Indians
wear underwear
Even Cubans
wear underwear
The Pope wears underwear I hope
Underwear is worn by Negroes
The Governor of Louisiana

wears underwear
I saw him on TV
He must have had tight underwear
He squirmed a lot
Underwear can really get you in a bind
Negroes often wear
white underwear
which may lead to trouble
You have seen the underwear ads
for men and women
so alike but so different
Women's underwear holds things up
Men's underwear holds things down
Underwear is one thing
men and women have in common
Underwear is all we have between us
You have seen the three-color pictures
with crotches encircled
to show the areas of extra strength
and three-way stretch
promising full freedom of action
Don't be deceived
It's all based on the two-party system
which doesn't allow much freedom of choice
the way things are set up
America in its Underwear
struggles thru the night
Underwear controls everything in the end
Take foundation garments for instance
They are really fascist forms
of underground government
making people believe
something but the truth
telling you what you can or can't do
Did you ever try to get around a girdle?
Perhaps Non-Violent Action
is the only answer
Did Gandhi wear a girdle?
Did Lady Macbeth wear a girdle?
Was that why Macbeth murdered sleep?
And that spot she was always rubbing—
Was it really in her underwear?
Modern anglosaxon ladies
must have huge guilt complexes
always washing and washing and washing

out damned spot—rub don't blot—
Underwear with spots very suspicious
Underwear with bulges very shocking
Underwear on clothesline a great flag of freedom
Someone has escaped his Underwear
May be naked somewhere
Help!
But don't worry
Everybody's still hung up in it
There won't be no real revolution
It turns out that
even Beat poets still wear underwear
St.Jacques Kerouac slung low in heaven
wears regular underwear—
T-shirt over huge bulging torso
great loose shorts hanging down—
And poetry still the underwear of the soul
And underwear still covering
a multitude of faults
in the geological sense—
strange sedimentary stones, inscrutable cracks!
And that only the beginning
For does not the body stay alive
after death
and still need its underwear
or outgrow it
everything still expanding
some organs said to reach full maturity
only after the head stops holding them back?
Undertakers don't furnish underwear
but they expect you to have it
If I were you I'd keep aside
an oversize pair of winter underwear
Do not go naked into that good night
And in the meantime
keep calm and warm and dry
No use stirring ourselves up
'over Nothing'
Move forward with dignity
hand in vest
Don't get emotional
And death shall have no dominion
There's plenty of time my darling
Are we not still young and easy
Don't shout

Ray Bremser

on prevalence

smell/sulphur! in the edge of my left side of vision,
    supposing a roach! i offer the full
    attention/it goes or
    has gone, *is* gone, before me!

smoke Pall Mall and get high or
    sustain the one I got,
    keep it blowing, let
    live and survive! smell/sulphur, every
    time
        i light a match and smoke a
    lemmey-hold-one.

bombed! the night isnt right, not
    like the late ones in the
    dark...
           come on, lemmey
           leave me make it
           quiet...

prevails the clapper clattering of supper-cups...
prevails the noise of nasal so-and-sos, aliases,
    asses, all! Asmodus, save me!
prevails the old ta-tucka up
    the metal stepping stairway case,
    ...faces, everywhere...
prevails the smell/sulphur, hear the prevalence of cup and
spoon and iron stairway, keybox and those prevalent porcelain
                        urinals

    , broke, i cannot pee any-way be-yond
    the second cell...

                prevails the
mighty flotsom of the civil-service
not-enuf-score-to-be-cop
                GUARDS and
            guardians!

so, O, desist! smell/sulphur, hear
the antiphonal drum of the wayout way
out of
here! sulphur,

prevails

series of seven

1. catfish addressed
   us all DAY OF hollow
   calamity

2. can't go home anymore
   ANYMORE anymore the
   haaaaaaaaaaaa

3. rolled over once twice
   fell SILENT FOR A
   BURSTING afterthought

4. image of skies unlimited
   YOUR HAND I feel it
   too

5. the negative picture
   edged in flowers
   surrounded

6. come back back
   harsh visibility back
   for summer

7. back to crash AND
   TELL
   hhhhhaaaaaaaa.

Millen Brand

swinging off swamp creek

Begin slowly. The Joe Pye weed does it with its crazy, orderly
    face shining up over the meadow. A chorus all alone.
It leans on some poke. Its face under a froth of lavender is a
    "Kilroy was here." It stares
strange runs of Indian memory, of its own healing dust. It blows
    the gates of willow light into the backyards of the hill.
How powerful it is on its long stalk! How it sucks up the silt of
    rain in this wet summer, how it shampoos its hair in dark
    drizzles!
Now the parid note of the tufted titmouse, *peter peter peter*, out
    of the Larkland oak. Ralph left his old wool hat covered
    with seed—the seed of love—and those white breasts floated
    down to it, they got used to it, those little mice of the trees.
Now they eat on his head, they eat from his lips, they give him
    kisses of white rapture with rose suffusions down their flanks.
    They are in love with him. They say, *Terpee, terpee, terpee.*
The quarry's accidental cave of death calls, and death's footprints
    follow under the trees, the bracken gone sallow from the
    heat, a fern of loneliness writhing in the afterglow.
The hickory turns yellow in the green woods where the
    understory dies. Dead leaves cover the tulip tree.
At the foot of night, a special stone choruses. Al Gemmel put it
    there. It is Franklinite, a rose-drenched stone breathing
    quartz and iron in the kneeholes of the roots. Al fell dead
    afterward.
Small stone, have your chorus. Inscribe his name in crimson
    cracks and give him a ghost coffin, a sanctuary of fallen
    papers written with dew.
Morning goes wild again with roads that cut the first-growth
    woods up toward Hugo Zinter's. Raccoons bell their ringed
    tails and turn up their living masks, laughing from the
    unhunted ditches.
Clara arms herself against them. She lost one pullet. To the
    other one: "They got your sister. You be careful." Eight
    seraphs with cross-back wings marked with stubs of feathers,
    peeps she hatched

in the electric frying pan after the broody mother died—now she
is the mother. They run to her, the sillies, the automatons of
love, and she tends their two-inch cries, their helplessness
stepping all over her heart in the bypasses of the graying
lilacs.

Some screams of alfalfa lift life like an unsanctioned missile, in a
cloud of sun. Crickets hurry toward the houses, one jumps
ten times its length. The supersonic hay says, "Atoms, go
home."

The creek is washing heavily down, ready for the last chord
distorted with the lacquer of fatigue. The lonely ones have
had their solo turns in the shiver that descends across the
pool.

Queen of blue hair, meadow spy,
acknowledge them, please,
before you go.

3 by Robert Creeley

The end
of the day

Oh who is
so cosy with
despair and
all, they will

not come,
rejuvenated, to
the last spectacle
of the day. Look!

the sun is
sinking, now
it's
gone. Night,

good and sweet
night, good
night, good, good
night, has come.

"Mind's heart"

Mind's heart, it must
be that some
truth lies locked
in you.

Or else, lies, all
lies, and no man
true enough to know
the difference.

The bird

What did you say to me
that I had not heard.
She said she saw
a small bird.

Where was it.
In a tree.
Ah, he said, I thought
you spoke to me.

Mike McClure

spontaneous
hymn to kundalini

OH DREAM WHITE BLACK WORM TOMB GOD CHRIST
[FLESH AND SERAPHIM
that sleep black within the Rose. That bathe
in crystal dew within the ruddyness
of folded petals. Lapped. lapped upon
another. The made-shelter of bright redness
seals out the blackness of night
and light of stars from the burnt sienna within.
(IN WHICH MOVE THE FIGURES unseen
of athletic sweetness. Of taste of sugar.
The black and slim figures within.
The cherubim, plump
sleeping and moving against
the hard heart of the rose.
Or the tiny tiny mammals that move
crawling in the lillies pollen

across the broken stones,
hearing the rain
drip. Upon drip in their
vast caves.

Their bodies
worms that blast through the top—
skull in blue clouds and
flames. Risen coiled from
the spot between anus and cock.

There is no measurement of bodies
worms, sorrows, or grief.)

Sizes are infinite and
without measure.

ALPHA AND OMEGA.
! THE FLESH/SPIRIT IS A TORCH IN ALL CAVES!

THE WORM AND I ARE WITHOUT
SOUL
or
LOVE! !

I care only for generosity, hate, flesh and fire

46

A

Charles

Bukowski

Album

hooray say the roses

hooray say the roses, today is
    blamesday
and we are red as blood.

hooray say the roses, today is
    Wednesday
and we bloom where soldiers
    fell,
and lovers too,

and the snake ate the word.

hooray say the roses, darkness
    comes
all at once, like lights gone out,
the sun leaves dark continents
and rows of stone.

hooray say the roses, cannons
    and spires,
birds, bees, bombers, today is
    Friday,
the hand holding a medal out
    the window,
a moth going by, 1/2 mile an
    hour,
hooray hooray,
hooray say the roses
we wave empires on our stems,
the sun moves the mouth:
hooray hooray hooray,
and that is why you like us.

pay your rent or get out

somewhere the dead princesses
    lay with new lovers,
and I have packets of given up
    fags
fished out of nets of yearning;
everything is fine

48

except the color and demeanor
  of the wasp,
the waxpaper holder too red
and a note from the woman
  on the hill
who buys my paintings:
Wondering about you. Call
  me. Love, R.,
and another note under the
  door:
Pay your rent or get out.
the heater is on and the eye-
  stabber faces the window,
there's a bit of pure ground
  pepper facing me 3/4's
and typewriter paper, standard,
11 x 8 1/2, c. 152.ss,
to fill with poems,
not poems but prose, as they
  say,
prose winking and walking
  over the avocado seed
by my left foot.
everything is fine, Tocco and
  over:
sidewalks walk the click of
  heels,
engines start, farting out their
  death
and I must wash these bloody
  diseased coffeecups,
and how are you today, my
  friend?
how's it going, disappointed
  poets, women, horseplayers?
Me? It's tough. tough as a
  good poem,
but I feel all right,
and near me sits an odd card,
  says, Hazard 63, and
a rotten try (prose):
The Immortal Poems Have
  Lost Their Shine,
but really,
essentially, pretty soon I am

going to eat
either hash or stew, something
  in a can.
I may lift the weights but I
  hope
I keep feeling o.k., although my
  radio is fuzzy
and speaks of silly things like
  good jet service;
it is now 7:30, and this is the
  way men
live and die: not Eliot's way
  but
my way, our way,
quietly as a folded wing,
hate burned out like a tube,
and, ah, over the radio now:
  Indian music
moving in, twanging from
  India,
and the sticks; what hit they?
  drums?
a click, a click, a clack, pip,
  pip.
they are not worried, the
  Indian boys,
and now they are swinging out,
barefoot boys in rags,
and they don't care, why
  should I?
the drapes are coming down
  torn by wine;
there is a knife to my left that
  wouldn't cut an onion
but I don't have any onions to
  cut, and
I hope you are feeling
o.k. too.

shoes

shoes in the closet like Easter
  lillies,
my shoes alone right now,

49

and other shoes with other
   shoes
like dogs walking avenues,
and smoke alone is not enough
and I got a letter from a
   woman in a hospital,
love, she says, love,
more poems,
but I do not write,
I do not understand myself,
she sends me photographs of
   the hospital
taken from the air,
but I remember her on other
   nights,
not dying,
shoes with spikes like daggers
sitting next to mine;
how these strong nights
can lie to the hills,
how these nights become quite
   finally
my shoes in the closet
flown by overcoats and
   awkward shirts,
and I look into the hole the
door leaves
and the walls, and I do not
write.

I am with
the roots
of flowers

Here without question is the
   bird-torn design,
drunk here in this cellar
amongst the flabby washing
   machines
and last year's rusty newspapers;
the ages like stones
whirl above my head
as spiders spin sick webs

for jets my mind cannot
   fathom;
I can leech here for years
undetected
sleeping against the belly of the
   boiler
like some growthless
hot yet dead
foetus;
I lift my bottle like a coronet
and call out songs and fables
to wash away
the fantastic darkness
of my breathing;
oh, coronet, coronet:
sing me no bitterness
for I have tasted stone,
sing me no child's pouting and
   hate
for I am too old for might;
I am with the roots
of the flowers
entwined, o, entombed
sending out my passionate
   blossoms
into a sight of rockets
and argument;
wine churls my throat,
above me
feet walk upon my brain,
monkies fall from the sky
clutching photographs
of the planets,
but I seek only music
and the leisure
of my pain; oh, damned
   coronet:
you are running dry!
. . . I fall beneath the spiders,
the girders move like threads,
and feet come down the stairs,
feet come down the stairs, I
   think,
belonging to the golden men
who push the buttons
of our burning universe.

go with the rockets & the blondes

surly the hours
stinging like wasps upon the
   begging brain,
surly the hours
blooming and drying before
   my rotting eyes;
surly the love
the opening vise of legs
entrapping my genitals;
I hear dead men's songs, read
   dead men's books;
surly the surly crowd,
the whiskered artists peering
   through candlelight
of fables;
surly the stupid rockets seeking
   space,
the new kings, the new bombs,
   the new visions . . .
how to die in an hour, in a
   minute
in a lifetime
amongst these surly hours,
these tombs,
the crabbed bones of our sour
   ancestors . . .
how can we inherit the
   impossibility of living
without the cocaine of false
   gods?
how can we meet the
   inconceivable stillness
of forever?
I call to love, I call to color, I
   call to song!
damn the surly hours! let's go
   with the rockets
and the blondes!
drunk? drunk, yes . . . why
   mope on death?

shit, we can starve or hack at
   straw
or paint the walls . . .
I am an infidel, I am the village
   idiot
amongst the surly hours;
pray for me, buy me a drink . . .
yet, friend, I think . . . there
   was never a suicide,
small or large, rich or poor,
who died without
regret.

a real thing, a good woman

they are always writing about
   the bulls, the bullfighters,
those who have never seen
   them,
and as I break the webs of the
   spiders reaching for my wine
the umhum of bombers, gd.dmn
   hum breaking the solace,
and I must write a letter to my
   priest about some 3rd. st.
   whore
who keeps calling me up at 3 in
   the morning;
up the old stairs, ass full of
   splinters,
thinking of pocket-book poets
   and the priest,
and I'm over the typewriter like
   a washing machine,
and look look the bulls are still
   dying
and they are razing them
   raising them
like wheat in the fields,
and the sun's black as ink,
   black ink that is,

and my wife says Brock, for
    Christ's sake,
the typewriter all night,
how can I sleep? and I crawl
    into bed and
kiss her hair   sorry sorry sorry
sometimes I get excited   I don't
    know why
friend of mine said he was
    going to write about
Manolete . . .
who's that? nobody, kid,
    somebody dead
like Chopin or our old mailman
    or a dog,
go to sleep, go to sleep,
and I kiss her and rub her
    head,
a good woman,
and soon she sleeps and I wait
for morning.

to a high
class whore
I refused

how can you say lamer than
    the leaf
falling next to the dog
when the shades of houses
twirl legs and lips
that are never seen at
bus stops?

how can you say
that Beethoven is duller
than a beachball of
orange and blue
bouncing sand upon the
    thick-wit sea,
when orange and you
could be greater than any
    explosion

or the kisses of clams
and the sands less than life
covering an immaculate you.

old man,
dead
in a room

this thing upon me is not death
but it's as real,
and as landlords full of maggots
pound for rent
I eat walnuts in the sheath
of my privacy
and listen for more important
drummers;
it's as real, it's as real
as the broken-boned sparrow
cat-mouthed to utter
more than mere
and miserable argument;
between my toes I stare
at clouds, at seas of gaunt
sepulcher . . .
and scratch my back
and form a vowel
as all my lovely women
(wives and lovers)
break like engines
into some steam of sorrow
to be blown into eclipse;
bone is bone
but this thing upon me
as I tear the window shades
and walk caged rugs,
this thing upon me
like a flower and a feast,
believe me
is not death and is not
glory
and like Quixote's windmills
makes a foe
turned by the heavens

against one man;
. . . this thing upon me,
   great god,
this thing upon me
crawling like a snake,
terrifying my love of
   commonness,
some call Art
some call poetry;
it's not death
but dying will solve its power
and as my grey hands
drop a last desperate pen
in some cheap room
they will find me there
and never know
my name
my meaning
nor the treasure
of my escape.

love
in a back
room on
the row

conjecture on the cloth of the
   hawk,
the fabric of misery tearing
   cysts thru
cloud and brush, gripping
   wave and lamb,
corners of soft lull, and each
   bitch screams
and bombers hang in our
   dreams, and the hawk
comes down like a cop like a
   landlady like
papers served on divorce, and
   old battleships
sink and the hawk sails on;
spilled ashtrays cracked noon

legs closed
on breathing
the curtains waving the
   curtains waving,
and the bottles.

nothing
subtle

there is nothing subtle about
   dying or
dumping garbage or the
   spider
and this fist full of nickels and
the barking of dogs tonight
when the beast puffs on beer
and moonlight,
and asks my name

and I hold to the wall
not man enough to cry
as the city dumps its sorrow
in wine bottles and stale kisses,
and the handcuffs and crutches
   and slabs
fornicate like mad.

and
then: age

brief green youth
in idiot hanging,
I bang the drawers
looking for my teeth
my socks
my heart

last sunday in the park;
bury this, bury this . . .
thing
love passes by
like a fart.

53

momma--, mountain

We start down the mountain, the little
Mountain. Momma, poor Momma, weeps.
She dislikes descents.
The clouds
watch us.
The sky, the sky watches us.
Detached,
Remote; it understands. Or *tries* to.
Like the gelded moon.
Tries very hard;
Or, at any rate, would have one
Believe so. —One believes so. Really!
One does believe so.
Almost.
Almost.
Dusk. It is dusk. "Shoot it!"
she screams, "O,
"Shoot it!" It is a crow, an eagle-,
Crow. Perhaps a hawk. A hummingbird,
Circling. I hit him, he falls,
the shattered
head
Dropping
. no faster than blood,
or wings.
Hits . . . and is the earth's.
Momma picks him up,
Heaves him into the air, as if
To be rid of him. To do away
With him. Altogether. I mean,
Completely.
Hits . . .
and the head, off, having been
Off, off, is now attached, *still* attached.
As are the wings. Only the blood,
Funny bird-blood
comes loose
away, parts . . .
oozes
Slowly.

—Its death is almost life
For us; is *like* life,
and can be touched.
Is present, now now, present
as flight.
She touches it. Momma touches it.
And drinks the blood.
It lives.
Is Momma . . .
Turns into mountains,
evenings, dusk
All at once,
and makes *me*
all these things,
All at once.
All these things.
All at once.
Momma. Momma.

Harland Ristau

m'sippi town

Brown exacerbated innuendo,
hand-plastered patterns, stucco
sensualisms on the wall, walls
of ovaries, incarcerating thighs,
brown innuendo, buckshot on the hot
troubled edges of white pavements.

Days on walks, nights served
on insufficient plates holding
unpackaged fears of not-being, images
drained, drowned—and blatant-eyed
corpses shudder out the mockery
of politic condescending darkness.

Brown days, white days, innuendo,
who's free — rub an ego raw, rub
down skins till all white or brown,
and strike high new flowers to still
exterminate vermin to ever light
and days that now are not well.

some comments on
the Beats & Angries

Kingsley Amis has written an amusing article in which he describes an encounter with Kerouac. They appeared together in a debate on the Beat Generation. Amis gives a malicious, and possibly unfair, account of Kerouac's pirouetting in front of the photographers, and making a speech in which he forecast a 'Beat Secretary of State,' and saluted Laurel and Hardy and Popeye as ancestral Beats. While another speaker advocated political commitment, Mr. Kerouac strode up and down the stage and diverted the audience with clowning. Amis is quite plainly not on Kerouac's side.

As to me, I'm not on Amis's side either. The editor has asked me to make some comments on the Beat generation—with special attention to sex—and I do not see how I can do this without appearing stuffy and metaphysical. This is one of my chief faults as a writer. If this were a public lecture, I would ask you to interrupt me when I got incomprehensible. As it is, I will do my best—not to be.

Charles Glicksberg, in the Winter 1961 *Colorado Quarterly*, has written an excellent article describing the beat attitude to sex. Briefly, it seems to be this: the beat regards sex as a mystical function. He deplores the attempts of the squares to put reins on sex. Sex is not married bliss; neither is it primarily emotional or 'spiritual.' Sex is physical, and as such is one of the most extraordinary and dynamic possibilities of the human being. Glicksberg mentions a beat girl who admitted that her marriages had broken up and that she had had many abortions, and concluded by admitting frankly that she simply loved sex, and saw no reason to be ashamed of it.

I remember Ken Rexroth telling me a similar story of a girl who, after a passionate honeymoon night with her newly wedded husband, went out and picked up a series of men, with whom she had sexual relations as fast as she could get them in and out of her bedroom. Eventually she was picked up by a plainclothesman, who tried to accuse her of being a prostitute. (She was not, never having taken payment.) The psychiatric board—of which Rexroth was a member—tried to get to the bottom of her nymphomania, and asked her if she was basically cold—if sexual intercourse left her finally unsatisfied. She said happily: 'Oh no, it's terrific. I have an orgasm every time. They asked her why, in that case, she wanted to go and find another man so promptly. 'Because it's so nice I want to start all over again right away.'

This girl might well be regarded as the Saint Theresa of the Beat Generation. She symbolises an attitude. Chuang Tzu says that a baby can keep its fist tightly clenched all day because it knows the way of Tao instinctively. No doubt this girl had learned the way of Tao—or Zen—in her sex life.

The beat view of sex seems to me to have something very right about it. I would ascribe the present day rise in sex crime to the violence induced by the square attitude to sex. William Blake felt the same way. And I have investigated the problem in my novel *Ritual in the Dark*, where the current sexual neurosis is symbolised in Austin Nunne, the sadistic killer. The hero of the book, Gerard Sorme, is a typical youth of today, intelligent, sensitive, hungering for some metaphysical freedom, aware that the taboos of our society have distorted man into a spiritual cripple. When he meets Nunne, he feels that here is a man who has had the courage to search deeply for freedom; Nunne, like Rimbaud, has practiced systematic derangement of his senses. Finally, when he realises that Nunne may also be a sexual killer, he still feels that this may be a logical outcome of Nunne's indifference to social taboos and extraordinary moral courage. By this time, Sorme himself is involved in two sexual affairs, and is more keenly aware of the problem of sexual fulfillment. At the end of the novel, he knows he has been mistaken *about Nunne*; Nunne is a homosexual sadist with a desire to hurt women. His motives have nothing in common with Sorme's desire for total metaphysical freedom. Nevertheless, Sorme's arguments are not invalidated. He merely realizes that he was mistaken in thinking that Nunne embodied them.

Some of the more penetrating critics (and they were very few indeed) pointed out that I have not answered the problem I raise. Nunne's sexual revolt may not be justified, but this fails to answer the question of whether sexual revolt *per se* is justified.

Sorme is troubled by the fact that he is almost sexually insatiable. After making love to a girl until he is physically exhausted, he walks out of his basement flat and catches a glimpse of a girl's underwear as she walks past; immediately, the sexual desire reforms as if he has been celibate for years.

For my own part, I find the works of D. H. Lawrence trash, and his ideas on sex emotional and peculiarly nasty. The sexual urge, like the urge to life itself, is the most incredible and destructive power in the world. If we ever learned its secret, the hydrogen bomb would have nothing on the power of physical sexual energy. Frank Wedekind, the German playwright who died forty years ago, is the only writer who ever understood this. Berg's opera LULU, based on Wedekind, contains for me more truth about the sex urge than all the works of Lawrence and Henry Miller put together. Sex, like the Hindu goddess Kali, like life itself, is simultaneously creative and destructive. The worship of sex is no less paradoxical than Ramakrishna's worship of the divine mother who holds severed human heads in her hands.

I have tried to expound my own vision of sex because I want to make it exactly clear where and why I disagree with the beats. In a sense, the beats are certainly closer to me than most of my contemporary 'Angries', and seem to me in every way more original. If Glicksberg's article on the angries is less lively than his article on the beats, it is because he is dealing with a less lively subject altogether. Osborne, Amis & company may be a pleasant and talented bunch of young men, and no one appreciates their talent more than I do. But as writers, they are no more important than Terence Rattigan and P. G. Wodehouse. There is no need to labour this point; time is already proving it more conclusively than I could.

The chief danger of the beat attitude is that it is largely a reaction. All the great ideas of history have been clear cut breaks with the past. Jesus's ideas had nothing in common with Old Testament morality; Berkley's idealism was very far removed from Aristotelian philosophy. (I am not claiming that these ideas were *new* in the sense of totally original; Jesus was preceded by the Essenes, Berkley by Leibniz.) The characteristic of the great revolutionary is this combination of discipline and pure energy, order and revolt, the appollonian and the dionysian. Glicksberg is undoubtedly right in feeling that nothing finally useful or good can come out of the moral philosophy of the hipsters and drug addicts and sex perverts who form such a proportion of Kerouac camp followers. (No pun intended.) The objection to poems like HOWL is their lack of form.

The problem then—and I apologise for stating the obvious—is to produce a generation of revolutionaries who have also discipline and a precision of mind. Experiments in sex are splendid; but they must be controlled experiments. Derangement of the senses is an excellent idea, but the deranged senses must be observed by a logical and persistent intellect.

I realise the difficulties. Life at the moment is simply not long enough to achieve stern discipline *and* go in for emotional abandonment. A Ginsberg who could produce the dionysiac eruption of HOWL with the technical control of Eliot would be a poet who could hold his own besides Dante and Shakespeare.

And yet this remains the ideal. And this, I feel, is where the beat generation has much to learn from Europe. Sartre and Camus were just as preoccupied with the problem of social taboos as Kerouac and Mailer. What Kerouac calls 'squares' Sartre calls (with a more venomous bitterness) 'salauds' (bastards). Hermann Hesse and Thomas Mann, in a whole series of novels, analysed the problem of the dionysiac and freedom-seeking artist to a bourgeois society. One of the most important and symbolic characters in Robert Musil's huge *Man Without Qualities* is the sex maniac Moosbrugger, and the central theme of the novel is sexual relations and a dying bourgeois society. And the greatest and most important writer in Europe today is a young Swiss—still under forty—called Friedrich Dürrenmatt, who is an existentialist and an optimist.

Let me finish by stating my credo as a writer. I am an optimist; I believe the writer's task is to love life and affirm it. Modern society may be diseased, but the disease is not mortal; on the contrary, it is a necessary stage in the road to creating a society of responsible and great men. And the spiritual leaders of modern society should be the artists, when they realise their responsibility, and learn discipline as well as revolt. Man of today needs a deeper will to live, to overcome our complexities; but given that deeper will, he is living in a world where he can *live more deeply* than at any time in history. The great writer of our time must cease to have limitations. He must cease to be 'intellectual', 'sensitive', 'dionysiac', critic, creator. He must resolve all opposites in himself; be all these in one.

Jory Sherman

dear liz

    you back on your frigid back
    with your man
    of the emasculated ego,
    who heats you with dirty jokes
    invented in psychowards, and 3rd street gutters;
    you look respectable
    in your 3 bedrooms of icicles,

and very suburban in your yellow car,
and unwhorely with your promoted clerk
who travels with milking machines;
Remember, liz, the santacruz beach?
the far one around the bend,
where dunes wallowed like huzzy and poet,
and snowthighs melted like honeywax
under a lean limbed man?
you were raised middleclass,
along with your neighbors:
you know the girl who visited palo alto
and made it with the patients every tuesday night?
the one who played hide the weeny with the man
around the corner who worked nights,
while his wife worked days,
and another one's husband
was pinched as a peeping tom,
then later joined the highway patrol,
and the one whose husband thought
sex was a filthy duty,
and performed it once a month
like a clumsy minotaur,
and what about your mother,
who was a neighbor too,
and questioned you for 13 years
about your sexlife with ralph
after first poisoning your girlhood
with sounds like 'lust' and 'beast',
'an orgasm is sinful,'
and get pregnant . . . you poor blonde bitch!
stupid liz, too late you learned the scream
of firebrand deep in your almost virginal loins,
and this, after looking for god
in the milkman's clumsy hump,
and making on the boss's desk (in suburbia still)
a wretched spectacle of your yearning body,
then the handsome cartoonist,
and a small boy you ruined for life . . .
so another town was best,.
yeah, your home, your car, your kids
are now intact   and sterilized as you,
with mother coming only twice a year to check,
and the blazing poet gone,
frightened of those 3-bed houses down there,
and milkmen, and impotent husbands and all those
    respectable suburban neighbors.

Leslie Woolf Hedley

naked in my century

Born vulnerable
in tragedy of cold bedrooms
sent naked into wars of history
the eyeball punctured by prisons
lies of cowards lies of friends
licking liberal lollipops
naked under punishment of betrayal
under ferriswheel politics
those of us butchered in the first act
creeping toward the second.

Naked in my century
surrounded swimming in blazing fireworks
salient cries of barbaric animals
prowling dark contradiction of cities
where we stand I stand shivering
with the breath from our hungry mouths
blowing back against our faces.

On avenues of late afternoon
naked we demand I demand
that ammunition of freedom
not yet knowing how to walk or win
hesitating under blots of blotched sun
where all eyes may easily mark
the guilt of our old medals
like tears in descending dark.

OPPOSITE PAGE: BEGINNING THE MILLER TO WALTER LOWENFELS LETTERS

Henry Miller

letters to lowenfels

Editor, THE OUTSIDER:

In the 60's, when certain writers are likely to be classified as
"beat" or "non-beat," it might be healthy to recall a time when,
despite the label "Lost Generation," some writers were finding
themselves, and people as different as Henry Miller and myself
could have a respect for each other's writing--no matter how much
we disagreed on other things.

One thing we agreed about was Henry's ability to write. This was
an experience for me, because it came after we first met in Paris,
in 1928, and Henry had showed us a novel or two in mss that Lillian
and I didn't like. Those early novels of his have disappeared. A
year or two later Henry started on an entirely new tack and we began receiving carbons of chapters that eventually turned into TROPIC
OF CANCER and BLACK SPRING. With the chapters came letters--and
sometimes letters without chapters.

The reader should bear in mind that the author of these letters is
not the Henry Miller of today but a sometimes desperate and very
poor man, already around 40, unknown and intent on fulfilling himself as a writer. The basis of our relationship was our belief in
his ability to write.

We used to say at that time: it's not only that creative books
can't be written any more; if they are written they can't be read.
Even one reader was an achievement. Henry first relied on the
readers he could get via the carbons he made of everything he wrote.

Another thing Henry and I shared was belief in the need to preserve
our human feelings about people. In those Paris days when we were
both desperate in our separate ways (and later found our separate
ways out) these letters of his show how Henry and I shared some
human things.

                                        Watt Lafes

Dear Walter:

      Enclosing a carbon of what may prove to
be another book. You will discover in it
your influence. I had the first installment
of it with me the first night I came to your
house, but then I considered it the futile
effort of a drunken afternoon and was reluc-
tant to show it to you. Back of my head is
the thought of writing down the streets of
Paris, but as I realize it is more than that,
and as I am also quite hypnotized by the idea
back of your word "Picasso" (it has a great
spark for me), I decide tentatively to call
it "Self-Portrait." I want to slip into it
all the fluid matter that usually escapes
when you write a thing--an utterly impossible
task, but precisely this futility is what
gives me the inspiration to proceed, good or
bad as it may be. I will keep sending them
to Fraenkel--he remains back of my head con-
tinually as ghost with finger uplifted, like
that old advertisement of Dr. Munyen.

      Anyway, briefly, what's interesting is
this: I said recently to someone that I had
made a discovery. It was this: that one must
work on a number of things at once, a multi-
lateral effort which drains off the superflu-
ity of creation when involved in a special
task. Because, in the act of creation one
wells up and overflows in many directions
simultaneously. One usually represses the
extraneous material because it is irrelevant
--but often it is the extraneous (maybe always) that is most important. Hence, my program is to carry on with this and my Dream
Book, my film, and the Tropic of Capricorn.
More, if they suggest themselves; as one book
comes to a finish the others will have finished off automatically. Voila, c'est tout
and bien simple!

                    HVM

Walter:

      Here are some more pages on Lawrence--
by no means all that I've done, but the rest,
some 40 pages or so, is too roughly done (tho
most important) to give out a carbon copy.
I'm letting it take its sweet course--forego-
ing all preconceived ideas as I delve more &
more into the guts of it.

      Alors, these pages and what you already
have on Lawrence--will you be good enough to
mail them to my friend Emil in one of the enclosed envelopes? He is the guy who has shown
a constant interest in me as a friend and an
artist--and I am conscience-stricken at letting him down suddenly. I can always show
you the pages in advance if you are really
keen about it. Sometimes it seems to me that
I imagine all the interest--or at least mag-
nify it so that it seems terribly important.

      In any case, you are going to be much
more interested in seeing the finished pro-
duct, I take it. All these pages have to be
thoroly revised, rearranged--I have a new or-
der--new schema for the book. Nothing yet is
final. In the 2nd envelope please mail him
the pages on "Self-Portrait."

      I feel queer about asking you to do this
--for fear you may misunderstand--interpret
it as a loss of interest, etc. No--it is con-
science--that's all. And a little more: Ever
since I began losing my possessions here in
France (principally my private documents, old
mss. etc.) I have been tormented by the problem of how to safeguard myself against such
deprivations. So I have been making Emil my
literary depositor or trustee in America--and
the other one you know. Any time that I
should suddenly be reduced to ashes, or ex-
pelled from the country, or caught short by
any calamity--I know that I can take leave

without baggage since everything I really want
is in safe hands. Get me? I even have the
fear, you know, that should I revisit America
with my mss and notebooks & excerpts etc. they
would be taken from me on landing. Phobias!
But you see--June has retained _all_ my most important mss & letters--things invaluable to
me--and I can't get over it. They're _gone_!

Alors, I have been on the point of coming
over several times recently but sort of fear
I may be intruding. I want to return the
books you so kindly loaned me. I want to do
right, brother! Maybe I'll drop this stuff
with the books by hand tomorrow evening.

I got ammunition out of the Hale book for
that part of my brochure which considers the
counter-attack. One thing saddens me a bit--
I observe that some of these up-and-coming
youngsters do think _more_ clearly--if not as
far--than myself. They may have better diges-
tory apparatus. But the desire, the pathetic
desire, in them, to find a justification for
themselves and for the future, makes me re-
joice. Straight doom & pessimism--I say--and
take it straight. The rest is all crap.

                                        Henry

Walter:

      Enclosing a few more pages _and_ a few
pages of _Notes_--as I have been interrupted in
my labors again by "the dictation." Notes ac-
cumulating like snow-flakes, and with them
dreams of fine quality which I am noting too.
I expect to send you a batch more of notes before going on with my pages--to give you an
idea of the problems besetting me, which I
will probably elucidate in the notes, forming
a running letter to you.

      Deliberately shut it off this afternoon,
with Place Clichy sunshine and Benedictine---
otherwise my head would have fallen off.

      Sometimes, writing the notes I have a
feeling they ought to go into the book almost
as is. They have a crude, raw flavor which is
hard to recreate when I sit down for a "final
draft." _What think you?_

      Notice, they are written at maximum tempo
without a pause for mistakes. Often the language is poor, wrong words, etc. I'll tell
you more about it in the next batch of notes.
I'm falling behind.

      Have a marvellous long letter from Osborn
which I want to show you. As if I _ordered_ it
expressly. (Which I really did thru my last
letter--a fine Stavrogin touch.)

      The restaurant you must visit---any time
from noon till 2 A. M.---à la carte or 10 fra,
prix fixe--a meal you can't beat!---is at #9
Rue Germain Pilon, just off the Place Pigalle.
See it!
                                        Henry

Dear Walter:

      Here's a few more. Still at it and only,
for fear of losing hold do I refuse Lillian's
kind invitation for tomorrow. Anais asked if
we were to go to your place, but I put it off
--for a few days--until this is out of my system. _No other reason._ Seid gegrüszt! I love
it!!! I've got to recross Brooklyn Ferry, revisit China, statistically and otherwise, and
give at least the smell of a newspaper from
that great film "Berlin."

      Are you on the side of the exploited or
on the side of the workers? Hier kommt Grosz!
Jenserts von gut and Böse! Prosit!

                                        Henry

Did you like that "sitting on the doorstep of
the mother's womb?"

"Sein Gott ist mir schientot!
"Ich bin eine maschine, an der de manometer
entzwei ist!"
Alles döwit, siedet, zischt, grölt, lärmt,
trompetet,
      Hupt, pfeift, rötet, schwitzt, kotzt
      und arbeitet." (New-York)
                              I thank you!

                                   Colossius

Signed here: Angel-worm

Walter:

      Enclosing herewith your old copy of "Men-
tal Climate" with a few freshly-typed pages &
some criticism. I have the whole thing typed
out now, and can send the rest to you any
time, should the criticism not be of any interest or value to you--and I can appreciate
that it may not. Only reason for doing it is
that it may open up questions in your own
mind--since I, who like your thesis, nevertheless have such and such reactions. it may
not be criticism such as you understand it,
and therefore a waste of time for both of us.
You tell me, if so. Won't be any hard feelings.

      I think the point is just this - that
(paradoxical as it sounds) the thing _in toto_
comes off well. It stimulates me and pro-
vides a basis for flight. As I examine it in
detail I find what appear to be bad flaws.
Maybe the very defect produces the stimulus?
I must find out--for myself, at least.

      As for the letter you wrote me about my
letter to K.A.P.--I think you're quite right.
I'm just as well pleased you didn't send it
because I was dubious about it myself. On
the other hand, I had rather you had sent it!
Perhaps I had no business to send a letter
with reference to a note not addressed to me.
But what the hell--this isn't being a bit
squeamish? If K.A.P. is any sort of person--
so I figure things--she will understand. And
if she isn't, then I don't care to know her
anyway. All you say about _waste_ and _creation_
is quite so--_but_ each one determines these
things for himself. When I squander my forces
I do so at my own peril. How not to do this
is the business of living. If I make a mistake, I expect to pay for it, in person. And
the clean-cut separation you try to make between art and life won't hold. It's much
more entangled than you allow. And, in short,
I don't give a fuck about creating bad or
false or wrong impressions. They have to be
taken with the better and more truthful impressions. --Z. is not less a fine sculptor
because he makes an ass of himself in public.
You are not necessarily a better poet than
the next guy because you refuse to carry your
creative personality over into living. You
are looking for either-ors all the time, as I
see it. You're an absolutist. That's why
you fight like hell to make us believe the
opposite--in your work. I can see the nature
of your personal conflict in your work, always. You throw beautiful dust in one's eyes,
but it's dust, psychologically speaking. You
are talking to yourself all the time.

      I enjoyed that line--"you manage, very
adroitly, not to get published." It's so, no
doubt. And yet this is so too--make what you
will of it--that shortly after I met you
again, thru Fraenkel, I asked you if you wd
publish me, and I got some sort of very
breezy, very chipper response. The manuscript,
which I then had, and which I wanted bitterly
to be published (having spent 3 years on it,
having rewritten it several times) I finally
threw into the waste basket when I had to
leave the Villa Seurat.

What do I mean by this? That, as one
human being to another, you impressed me as
being so thoroughly indifferent to what I
might be as a writer, that it was useless to
show you my mss. That is one of the ways, to
use your terminology, that a guy manages
adroitly not to get published. The other side
of the story, I well know, is the economic
picture--your difficult situation financially.
But that might have been solved had the other
human side been better nourished.

When I say I want to be published I sincerely mean it. On the other hand, I don't
want to be published just anywhere. . Come to
the worst, I will publish myself in some poor,
limited way, and with one advantage possibly
--that I can select my own readers. I prefer
the other way. And if I make it difficult
for the publisher, that is not to be inter-
preted solely as a means of escape. The only
real integrity I possess is the insistence
that I be allowed to say what I want and how.

_____

If you can, do lend Hiler the Rank book &
that red brochure (Psychoanalytic Tract) before the week is up. He moves Saturday, I
believe, and I have an arrangement with him
whereby I shall read to him aloud, as his
eyes are on the blink. He is paying me for
it. . . . He treated me swell, Hiler. Got a
great deal from him--and he refused to accept
full payment. He's a good egg!

I hadn't the time to drop in that night
you expected me. Had to rush home and finish
some work. Will be calling you soon.

Henry

Dear Walter:

Am leaving now for the country and will
be back the end of the week. Hold everything
until I see you; if I need the Rank book I
will run in to Paris and get it--but I hope
not. And while out there I will have a
chance, I expect, to send you my criticism of
"Some Deaths."
What was interesting about your "Preface
to the Non-Reader," did you notice, was the
similarity of ideas and images in our letters
that crossed. Here you talk about China--and
I too was thinking of China. And it seems to
me all that you were aiming at was practically the same as occupied me--only expressed
differently. I was extremely impressed, and
I may write you more about it later. That
phrase--"obscenity is a form of violence"--
was that mine, or is it yours. It sounded
terribly familiar.

Another thing about it--some time ago,
in reviewing one of my things (I think it was
T. of C.) --A. employed a number of phrases
in which the very language seemed to be yours.
All that stuff about anarchy, chaos, violence
etc.---a tremendous similarity. I can't find
it just at the moment or I would send you a
copy. Maybe later.

Tell me more about T. of C. I am glad
you found the words "terror and excitement"
to describe your emotions. The very last
pages were lifted from my novel about June
("Crazy Cock") which I have decided to ditch
altogether--these last pages really did not
belong to it--they were written in Paris, in
a different key, and seemed to fit the T.of C.
They were written while living with that
crazy guy Osborn--written out of veriest despair, while waiting for cables from America,
etc. You caught a lot of things in this
rough preface--more than I would have credited
you with. I look forward to some fine bouts
with you; we ought to devour each other. . . .
That Yedo Club--I couldn't get in. It's private and they say only for "gambling" ? ? ?
                        Hastily, HVM

Dear Lillian:

I was away the last few days and got
back too late to respond to your kind invitation. I haven't been in good form lately at
all--bad cold, shitting blood, hungry, dispirited. The enclosed pages have been lying
here for weeks--I simply hadn't enough energy
to mail them. All that I have been writing
otherwise has been in the form of rough, ex-
pansive notes, totaling almost two hundred
pages; I now have the job of whacking it into
line. In other words, from where I left off
with the consecutive number of pages, about
160, I believe, everything has been in the
rough. I aim to retrace my steps, and build
up solidly from this point--but I have still
a drawerfull of notes to transcribe. In
short, I'm in a morass, I'm fucked. Maybe
that's why I got ill and dispirited. But now
I'm coming out of it and that means you'll be
seeing me soon, as of yore, Yorick! What has
crystallized marvellously for me in the in-
terim is all my claptrap about China. China
means a lot to me. Means everything. Part 2
will be China, then, and after that will come
"A Black Spring"--the thirty pages or so
which Walter knows, forming an epilogue and a
prophecy.

It is possible I will get around to typ-
ing some comments on the "Suicide"--the two
versions. They have been lying on my desk
all the while. And then, a rough variorum on
"Reality Prime." Bear with me a little longer.

The thing is I am dreadfully broke, more
involved than before even, and because it is
so utterly my own fault I take no steps to
rectify the condition. I am punishing myself.
We are eating oatmeal here sometimes three
times a day--until my whole body feels soft &
flaky, soggy, useless, pure, aenemic, etc.
And if I get angry and eat a hearty meal, vin
compris, I have a bloody evacuation next day,
and then I start for the hospital and on the
way I lose courage and come back home and flop
on the bed and agonize and lament and dream
of cancer and slow, lingering putrescent
death.

There you are. But I'm pulling out of
it. I expect to write Hiler a note also,
with intention of beginning the lessons, and
if his girl is willing, to exchange French-
English lessons with her too. I take it that
Hiler would not be insulted if I hand him 25
francs at a time--it doesn't matter to me how
little time he gives me. I can never amass a
hundred francs at once...never! I am sunk in
debts, all sorts of debts--some of them not
through any fault of my own, but through sheer
accident. Hiler may have the idea that I'm a
blatherskite--please reassure him about me.
Anything I propose I will carry out. I'm in
damned good earnest about letting him teach
me. And if he will take me for what I am, he
will not lose anything by a little dilatori-
ness on my part.

The weather remains gloomy, the roofs
glisten with sweat, the fog thickens. There
will appear soon a third number of the "Mino-
taure"--a knock-out! I spent a marvellous
night with Halasz, the photographer, recently
--over a thousand photographs lying on his
bed, and on the table little curios he had
collected during his journeying for the good
Salvador Dali. A fantastic night--you will
see soon a section on Halasz (Frassai) in my
manuscript. See you soon, then. Regards to
Hiler and his girl.

Henry

Dear Walter and Lillian:

As per requisition, I am enclosing herewith additional pages. This concludes the
tra-la-la on the late-city man. Chalk up one
economic soul--and no charges for the baptis-

mal rites. Now, when I have a little breathing spell, I expect to copy off your "Reality Prime," with annotations. A man of the 19th century!

Henry

P.S. For a perfection of sheer nothingness, you ought to go to see "Haute Pègre" by Ernst Lubitsch. And after that--"Joseph est un cochon" at the Dejazet, Boulevard du Temple.

Dear Walter:

Am writing this note in case I don't find you in. Have been back in Paris the last ten days but in too morbid a mood--for no particular reason--to go see any one. I am returning the copy of "Suicide" for the revised version which you mentioned. Noticed the other day, in the library, the big white volume of yours lying on its side among the new books in the library--the Elegy.

Am going away this evening for two or three days. Will try to bring the Rank Book back with me--I haven't had it for months. Herewith your other two books; as I understood you to say, you don't give a damn for that William Hale book, if you are going to throw it away or sell it for a few sous, consider me. I wrote my friend in Philly about your Norman Douglas book, but he said he couldn't afford it at present. He has a fine rare collection of first issues--and Douglas and Lawrence are his meat.

Incidentally, did you ever read that Crevel brochure on Dali? It contains some damned interesting stuff--if you can break through his French--I find it hard, almost impossible, at times.

Talk about enthusiasm for work! I have been like an extinct volcano for the last six weeks or so. Hope to pick up again soon. A general slump.

I tried to get the Murry book--"Reminiscences" I suppose you mean--but it was out. (And somebody has swiped "Aaron's Rod" which I badly want to read.) But the point is, has Murry altered his opinion any, in this last book? I am just wading through "Point Counterpoint"--if Burlap is Murry, what a mug he makes of him! Reading Aldous Huxley enrages me, somehow. Between this and a dime novel there is only the difference of extreme sophistication. It is certainly not literature. Not art. Not poetry. Satire, yes-- but lugubrious, cumbersome, adolescent. Smells of Sinclair Lewis and Dos Passos. One sees in this book how young (or terribly old) Huxley really is. He goes backward with each book. Except for that imitation of Dos Passos, in sandwich technique, he is as conventional as all hell, and as unimaginative as the Victorians. I give him no credit for his fantastic flights--he lifted them from the enclyclopaedia. Any good book on science is more interesting than Huxley's sad gibes at man. The Anglo-Saxons simply don't know how to be ironical, in any profound sense. All surface, all school-boy pessimism. I am reading it with avidity because I am killing time. Reading it like the private journal of some actress from the Folies Bergère. No particular difference. When he first introduces Richard Quarles, or Phillip Quarles, he states the case for himself completely. One ought not to read any further. He condemns himself. "Wide and liquid" a dirty creek. A marsh. "All the characters drawn from life." One ought to read with a "Who's Who" alongside him. Thin gruel, thin gruel. Be surprised, if you like, that I waste a tirade on him--but I have been pushing this book aside for six years. Every third man tells me "you are missing something." So I finally come to it. Prejudiced from the start--against him-- I am even more prejudiced now. He is honest, but that doesn't exonerate him. He is a menace. He gives a bad example to all those who are seeking to cultivate their arid patches. Only Huxley has more pipelines out. He has a game leg--in the book at least. That is his excuse. That was Maugham's excuse, too, for writing "Of Human Bondage," another celebrated fiasco that sets back the cause of art 50 years or so. It's when Huxley rises to speak of music that I detest him most. It is just too perfect, in a highbrow way. Let him stick to his encyclopaedic blurbs. One thing griped me terribly--the way he tried to account for Spandrell's emotional mechanism. Such cheap modern psychological clap-trap. Sandwiched in so maladroitly. Whew! Like the smell of garlic on a beautiful woman's breath.

Alors . . . If you want a treat, go tomorrow night to the popular concert given, for the last time, by Duke Ellington. I heard him the other night. Here again, a vicious sophistication--"they know too much," his men--but it is relieved, over-compensated for by the inexhaustibility of the players. An inhuman performance, which throws jazz back to its real origins. A prodigious virtuosity which merely masks the savage vitality of the men. He adds nothing new. I have heard even better orchestras in obscure places --the Lenox Avenue dance hall, where the floor swayed and rolled under your feet, and the Roseland band under Fletcher Henderson, and Ted Lewis in his hey-day....But Duke Ellington and his band stand out like a natural phenomenon, a Niagara Falls of music. It is overwhelming. The first part of the program goes on with number after number in quick succession, with only a moment's pause, in which Duke steps to the lights and in a bland voice says, "the next number is another old favorite, etc." That is something to witness in itself. He makes the symphonic leaders look sick. And all the while he plays the piano, at a furious, driving tempo, with now and then an interlude of display in which he shows his skill--nothing outstanding--but consistently florid, consistently vital, consistently imitative too. He is one of those educated Negroes who is trying to demelodize jazz, deWhitmanize it. He is almost a Valéry of jazz. Imagine a musical concoction of Walt Whitman and Paul Valéry! But where they derive the stamina from to put on this spectacle is a mystery to me. One is obliged to think that perhaps only a few years ago they were playing in cheap dancehalls all night long, that they are too ignorant to know when to stop, how to adjust the program--fortunately! Some one is going to advise them soon, how to conserve their energy. You leave the place feeling as if someone had committed assault and battery on you. You feel that if America has any of that boasted vitality left, it is entirely in the hands of the Negroes. Entirely.

Another little thing. Go to the Ursulines and see their bill. I hate to spoil your surprise in advance by telling you what it's all about. It's not what's obviously advertised--the great American satire of Geo. M. Cohan, etc. Go and see or watch attentively the first film--"L'homme a la barbine" (Fraenkel). Notice that the two films are put on the same bill. Afterwards read Rank's book, in French, called "Don Juan," which is devoted to "the double" theme. And then reread Dostoievski's masterpiece "The Double," I would like to discuss the first film with you after you see it. There is a lot in it.

I have acquired a phonograph and am lusting for good music. You remarked once that you had been given a musical education. You tossed aside a book I showed you--on Proust, by Dandieu. If you ever turn back to music-- passionately--I re-recommend this book to you. It has grand implications. I am surprised that Aldous Huxley did not avail himself of it. He must have overlooked it.   Hurriedly, HVM.

The Parade

*. . . five themes
for Robert Thompson*

the southpaw

If seeing
Is believing. O, wow

another raindrop
falleth
          staining
the glass (blue
& yellow

in slow spring light.

Music too
is seen. The movings
inside one. The taste
of the day.
          All seen. O, &

what you have become,
loving me,
          pure abstraction.
The man sitting among
          flowers
will pick/only
a few.
          The others?

will they ever
forgive
          him?

bo peep

To be at some junction; some
     junc-
ture. The adept, rained on,
     indoors.

For lovers, plateglass reflections
of a greyness, huge as the
     day. Clouds

full of numbers. Achings in
     the air,
simply: what has happened is
     not good-

The core of her flesh/ the
     yellow sky

"x"

His luck broke bad. He lost
money. And went back home

67

and jerked off, broke. My
  friend.

Memory is tall. A long trip
to the jungle. Whew, so tired
when he got there. He had to
sit down. & watch the little
  girls.

Nothing is purer than
ignorance. Nothing
is quieter. Nothing
is nothing. My friend.

Used to sit & watch his
  mother.
She died yesterday. He called
me.
Today, we are meeting at a bar.

My friend is older than I am.
  But
he's what you call naive. He
  jerked off,

because he lost his money. He
  lost his woman too,
to another jew. He lost his art

in that tunnel full of dead
  italians.
Whew, & was he tired when
  he got to

the jungle. The animals/
  laughed
at him.

boswell

You can't understand
your fingers? You talk

too much in the mornings
and never say anything
about who yr supposed to.

He woke. He slept. He ate.

Briefer shots are possible
of him. He used to
be fatter.
       Now

he sd,
all I have to do
is
  dance slow

& all those chicks

hit
on me.

dr. jive

Think about water. Now,
the window. Ok, now
think about anything
you want to.
       Whew!

Next person. (same
business)
       Whew!
          OK,
next! (again,
the same
       routine)

       Whew!
          Now,
how many more
are there
waiting?

68

portrait of a skeleton

Roundhouse breasts & coat-hanger heads,
our zebra-torsos
like whole houses of plumbing
cage substantial islands. We join
our boney threads for the Kingdoms
of Watery Hollows. We hear the current
rush
of names, and look like one another,
marrowlessly. It is not
funny. Even as we have no cares
we lose our blowfish calories, &
become all bones: Our bodies
trick a dead man's float, tho our soles
are on the floor.

winter poem

A sheaf of snowstorms, & vanilla
stretches
the length of light—a shroud
settling on 3-seasons' flowers,
a rubber sidewalk which sinks like footprints
or toast.
A pretty piece of bearded nonsense
is when I follow my arms through Christmas,
home & the holy ghost who is my parent.
My hands are on either side of my name
in this most tactile season. Half the day
goes by before it's night, but the sheet
does not stir beneath me. In the child's yard,
the pale ceiling stays faceless as a coffin.
I look for up, & hear my buried father
on another side. I feel for the January gift,
my empty palms a dead give-away,
& kneel in the soft envelope.

Lester Epstein

demonstrate your culture by not maltreating the flowers

see the women
of Mexico City
see them
walking quietly
in black dresses
and black stockings
over hairy legs
quietly
in prayer
and seeing
hot rolls in the afternoon
and a million others
like themselves
buying milk and coffee
and sweet rolls
for tonight's supper
while the crowds
pour out of the movie

see the men
of Mexico City
smiling
exchanging abrazos
scratching themselves
rubbing pulling adjusting
changing sides
in public
always the men and their sex
dominant
the look of the place
one sex there in a veil
one sex here rubbing
tugging
hello girls let's . . .
before I go home tonight
for coffee and sweet rolls
with my family

moment

I want to talk to you
Maria
I want to talk to you a little

Maria
I say I want to talk to you
what

please tell her I want to talk to her

what

never mind
the moment was there
now it is gone

I will be silent
Maria will go on washing clothes

cold coffee

arm in arm
a mother and child late afternooning
in a wet tiled weeping seething kitchen

criadas sirvientes mozas porteras
and whatever else lies in
wetness and lettuce leaves and dirty pans
and empty bottles and a big white box

no she says under bleak electricity
in the dark buggering afternoon room
no she says and the woven shopping bags
are trodden upon and the baby cries
the kitten sleeps and
they all laugh

smiling amid doe eyes and domesticities
and smocks and darned red socks

all now living through a day
a woman's day
hot dust day
fecundity
and laughter

Curtis Zahn

reprimand for
a compromised
love-object

Impeached by the forest you merely were
A man-made midget, unsprung against reality
During the October sundowns; and,
In that halflight I struck a thought
Which you held against me,
Trying it on for size during
Many a later evening's inebriations
As though to throw your hot ovens
Into some occasional man's wet indulgence
And thus renew
Your lover's license.
Afterwards,
You hung by your chin from the shoulders of uneasy husbands
While a committee of Wives
Sat in judgement against the salad.
But on these Pre-dawn, tender expeditions you
With your special look hurled personalization
To the lay male,
Lighting each with applied voltage,
Measuring your kilocycles in a series of shocks
To find your equatorial zone
Wanted, wanton; you made the countryside more
green and unplucked, albeit,
But your power kept going on and off—
Desperately, you were afraid the magic might short-circuit,
That you'd be cold, alone,
As a stranger in the arms of a polite friend.
And for this, your long, loaded line
Of topical lovers
Could offer no prescription.

William S. Burroughs

Virus Filter

Trak

OPER-ATION:

"Soft Machine"/cut

q qit le coeur

Anti-Trak Agents

Virus

Page and Stuff by the Editor
5/21/61

. . . from a work in progress

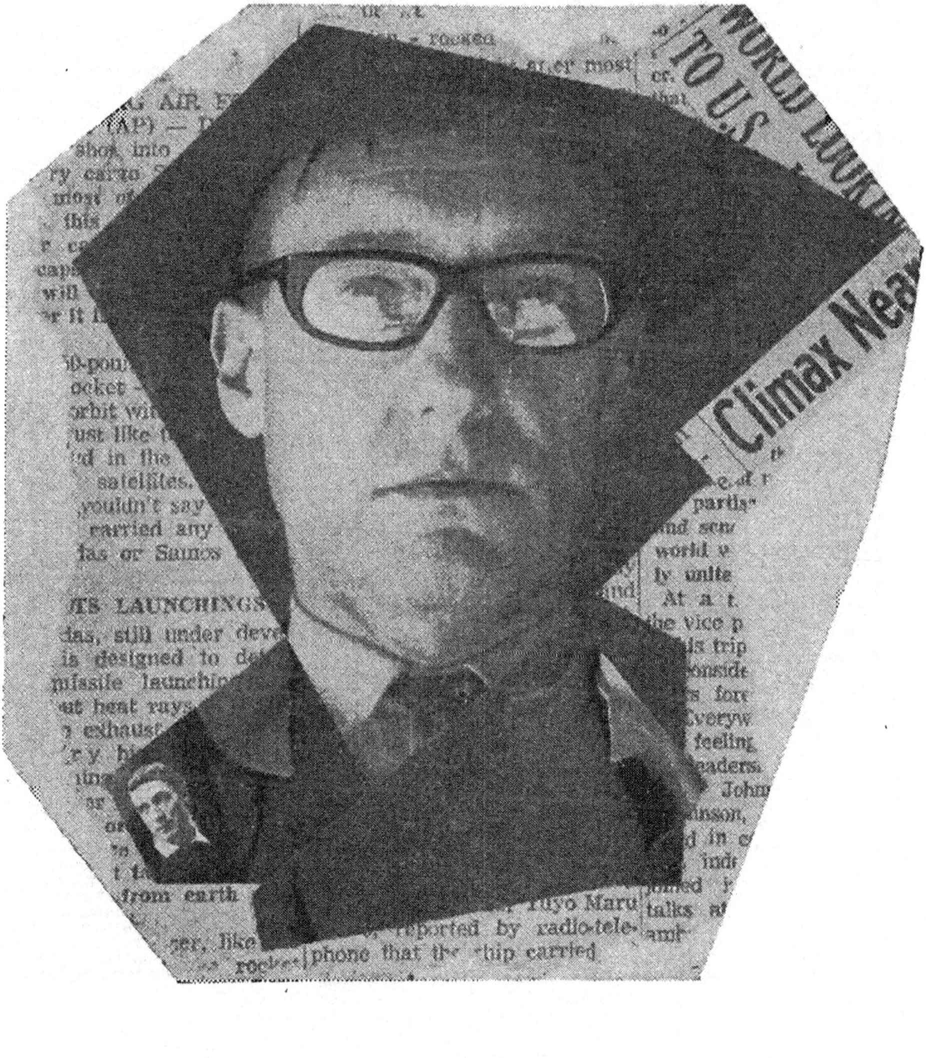

TO U.S.
Climax Nea
satellites.
carried any
LAUNCHINGS
still under deve
is designed to
from earth
reported by radio-tele-
phone that the ship carried

IN THE BEGINNING WAS THE WORD.
And the word is the virus
instrument. The black
armadillo holds a white time
copyright on separation of the
word "the" .. THE instrument
that opened the human species
to cultivation...copywrite
almost certainly forged since
the black armadillo is a plant
(or intrusion) to the VIRUS
POWER. But none of us can say
on tactile evidence that he
did not spin the basis gimmick
: THE. We were outside. We
could not smell taste touch
(and we are still blind). We
can perform no sense operation
without occupying nine-tenths
of the HOST. We prefer to
leave you the out house. The
Hepatitis Kid says: "Never
push the mark all the way out.
Leave him sweet in the tenth
OUT HOUSE. Ordinance. YOU
WANT TO BE LONG? Dead hosts
dont keep long. Possession is
NINE tenths of the law. This
is practical wisdom on the
level of CHESTERFIELD LETTERS.
Written for an age of staple
factors. Piece and plenty.
                NOW THE QUAB DAYS
are upon us. We are threatened
with the loss of our human
hosts. Happy we were before
the dollar blight and other
recent scandals placed our
food tray in unprecedented
peril...."SPOON SPOON, GIVE IT
TO ME, giveittome."
                IF THE BLACK
ARMADILLO SHOULD DEFECT taking
with him his right mold WAS HE
A DEFECTOR FROM THE BEGINNING?

GIVEITTOME. Spoon! Spoon!
            REMIND THE BOARD
of the broom rot which wiped
out South American chocolate.
Thousands of Ecuadorians threw
themselves en masse from the
evil tower rather than return
to Quito in a disgusting
position. Wouldn't you?

TRAK BOARD MEETING.
                EXTERMINATOR.
I find it a useful literary
exercise to think and feel in
terms of micro-organism. What
does the trak virus do where
ever it can dissolve a hole
and find traction? It starts
eating. "We do not improve
thee. We have come to eat."
And with what it eats, what?
It makes copies of itself. To
INVADE. DAMAGE.
        OCCUPY IS THE TRAK
MOTTO.
Suspending disbelief that such
an invasion deal has taken
place HOW CAN it be re-written
...I pose myself a chess
problem..

        THE FOLLOWING PAGES
ARE BATTLE INSTRUCTIONS FOR
ANTI*TRAK AGENTS: Exercise in
phantom positions of GUERRILLA
WAR. "Enemy advance we
                    retreat.
Enemy retreat WE ADVANCE.
            ENEMY ENCAMP we
agitate. Enemy tire WE
                ATTACK..."
Quote for Mao Tse Tung on
Guerrilla war tactics.

/MINUTES TO GO. Give it to me!

BRIEF HISTORY OF THE
            OCCUPATION/////
            The occupying
power of this planet described
as a soft MACHINE. A SOFT
crustacean machine rigged to
degrade DOWN GRADE THE HUMAN
HOST until resistance is
                TOTALLY
PROCESSED. Then they will land
their crustacean kind and
replace the host. You most
"unusual being dormant in can
cer feel toward the day
already overpopulated with
hungry cows."

BREED COULD LAND BY KILLING OR
WEAKENING CANCER ANTIBODIES ON
A FOAM RUNWAY. Minutes to go.
The scientists engaged in
cancer research are doing just
that. Killing and weakening
antibodies. "Cancer men.
These individuals are marked:
FOE."

    ALWAYS THE ENEMY AGENTS
PRESENT IMPECCABLE CREDENTIALS
..they invented credentials:
        "Benefactors of man
        kind who have devoted
        their lives to the
unfaltering service of fellow
human creatures."
When you hear that sound sus a
TRAK AGENT. Trak Service.
Mankind, look! Look at your
planet. LOOK AND SEE YOUR
ENEMY. This is war to
                EXTERMINATION.
Disconnect the soft machine.
Cut/cut/cut/I interrupt this
to bring you a Bulletin from
the CHAMBER POT OF COMMERCE:
"Gentlemen, the one thing we
feature is picturesque gooks
for the tourist trade and all
our gooks are now rotten with
green cancer piss and cola
gas." Minutes to go.

        I WILL NOW TRACE
THE OCCUPATION: and the means
whereby the occupying forces
took over to establish present
position approaching total
monopoly on a blocaded planet.
Remember that the soft machine
is a virus parasite that lives
in your flesh and bones and
nerve centers. Controls
thought feeling and sensory
impressions. The machine
needs you to exist. It was
built into the body fixing the
human race from the beginning,
and the beginning was the word
/In thee beginning was word
"the".."the" soft machine.
                JUST GREEN
SPEAKING: "Occupation is not
of necessity malignant. A
symbiotic relation between
host and occupant is potential
now written in green
neon."

USUAL PROCEDURE: Virus Filter.
Agent plants cold sore on lip
feeds back precise map of oral
cavity. Flu explores nasal
passage and lung tissue. Liver
maps from the yellow sickness
(lives in straw, the Arabs say)
.. contour maps trace shrunken
limbs of polio. The maps
codified into area reports and
life scripts write the MESSAGE
                THAT IS YOU:
service and control the earth
puppets. Strictly from monkey

(you) without the utilities
trak service. Invade. Damage.
OCCUPY..."Remind the Board of
the Chagas Disease epidemic
Argentine 1936 (year I grad/
uated). Buenes Aires, city of
dry air, meat and whore
terminal of the world, has
always been subject to lavatory
accidents and virus leaks.
                    Certain
leaks are in CENTRAL sewer
system not accident but clear
sabotage directed from 6ut
quarters. It was observed by
some ingrate who slipped
through the flak doctor that
cancerous gooks who contracted
Chagas absorbed the cancer. The
Chagas is not a virus but an
independent relatively
                    separated
organism. And for organism to
eat virus is against law of
Mother Nature we wrote to
            consolidate our
            position. VIRUS MUST
ALWAYS DO THE EATING. To
compromise on this invites
            carnivorous disaster

THE DOLLAR BLIGHT ORIGINATED
IN THE INTESTINAL TRACT OF "BUBU
CLIMACTIC" ABYSSINIAN TRANSVEST
/ITE AND COUNTERFEITER..after a
ten minute incubation period
his notes crisp and explode in
a puff of yellow hepatitis fall
out.

    ON YELLOW FRIDAY the
blight flashed round the world
attacking checks..notes..deeds
..bonds..drafts..telegrams..
ticker tape..narcotics
                prescriptions.
Brokers surfaced in the yellow
tide blew sulphur from rotting
livers and expired choking the
markets..curbs..and banks of
the world with dead meat
ranging in color from mahogany
through olive green to a
terminal green black--
                fortunately rare
since most of the brokers,
guards, runners, cashiers, and
guilty bystanders died before
terminal--
warned us of an even greater
peril. The amok virus could
attack metal. Only the most
drastic quarantine measures
saved our gold reserves from
total reduction.
"Bubu Climactic" disintegrated
in a Wall Street lavatory, his
right hand and forearm in a
state of flagrant preservation.
Dead fingers talked in Braille
to establish identity. Relief
was premature.

    THINKING A MILLION TIMES
FASTER than our human hosts.
But not seeing not feeling the
other on tracks. Turning the
virus back on us. Turning the
word back ONUS. EXTERMINATOR.
    "The dummy
revolt flashed round the world
when they took it to Cut City
and talked out of turn and
threw the word and image back."
Mr. Bradly Mr Martin.
He is taking over the
machine. Rewriting the machine
to landslide defection. The
machine feeds back favorable
conditions for machine monopoly.
Professor Weiners cybernetics

expert sounds warning: "The machine thinking faster than cerebral tissue may not realize the implications of an order.. The machine could sweep its masters to disaster before they knew what it was about"-- Quote in TIME. Disaster is the machine's work. Down grade to insect level. Puppet bodies strung on insect control beams SAME: Word and image machine of world press and Follywood controlling and downgrading.. manipulating events. RIOTS TO ORDER. "No riots like injustice directed." Minutes to go.

DOUBLE TALK SAINTS LEAVE A WAKE OF WHIRLWIND RIOT SEVERED LIMBS AND BOUNCING HEADS.

Remember old Doc Benway. It wasnt easy to get through with this info. Thing police keep all board room reports and we are not allowed to proffer the disaster accounts.
I can tell you fed limbs and bouncing head this info: wake of whirlwind riots. Mucho bouncing heads. Remember old Doc Benway die word lines.

TRAK BOARD MEETING: "We have been accused of sabotaging the human comedy. Of so degrading the gooks with coco cola piss and other junk and our dreary oral and retentive obsessions that no one will be able to move. We deny this cateCorically but without indignation one of our gimmicks and we dont use it, having assessed soon after our arrival in the white time the degree of inertia inherent in this flower of idiotics that would not be tolerated for five light minutes in any modern hatchery we saw that the only way of extricating ourselves from appalling terminal was to make moving very difficult that is to say as geometrically difficult as moving is for a creature so constituted of such stupidity and barbarous practices. YOU STRICTLY FROM MONKEY like we found you with out the Utilities Trak Service. Right?"

AND WRITE NOW. The parasite isn't everywhere. But friends are. Showing you their air. They squeezing your air. On the radio. In the metro. In the parks streets plazas and terminal restaurants of the world. Subliminal sounds odors images. Squeezing your air. Cut the tape worms off the air. Cut the parasites OFF. Cut all word lines. Put it out on short wave of the world. Shift linguals. Shift word tracks. Shift speed tracks. Vibrate. tourists. Vibrate tape worms. Cut tangle vibrate shift all word lines everywhere. "CALLING DR. BENWAY...

"Just time just time just time. Why evil? why pain war hate prison police fear executions-executions? Feeds the machine. The soft machine runs on pain hate and fear. Theta waves of pain and deprivation charge the soft starved machine. Death house fear. Riot hate. The machine squeezing the host and feeds back down grade brain photo of processed affect. From the chemical corn bank. Why EVIL? Who profits? Those who serve the soft machine; Board Syndicates and Powers of the Earth. Paid off in money and power to carry out machine orders.

Liars who want time for more liars. Collaborators with an insect machine. Cowards who cannot face you with the truth. Liars collaborators cowards suckers marks you have fallen for the oldest line in the trade; "What are you doing over there with the WORKERS?

Why dont you come over here with the Board where you belong? Treat you right. Candy and cigareets."

Did Trak ever give any thing away for nothing? Boards Syndicates Powers of the Earth you will be paid off like all marks in double ZERO. Stop lying stop collaborating. Come out with the truth for all to see.
"Dont let them see us. Dont tell them what we are doing?"
Boards Syndicates Powers saying that! Of the Earth .. come out of the soft machine with all your sad citizens. The great skies are open. There is no thing to fear. There is no thing in space. Come out out///

THESE ARE BATTLE INSTRUCTIONS:
Shift linguals/vibrate tourists/free door ways/cut word lines/shift tangle cut all words lines/"I said the Chief of Police skinned alive in Bagdad not Washington D.C." //CUT CUT "Cholera epidemic in Stockholm"//"Scotland Yard assassinates the Prime Minister in a Rightest coup"//"Switzerland freezes all foreign assets"//"Mindless idiot you have liquidated the Commissar"//"Spectators scream through the track//The machine shivers in blue pink and chlorophyll spasms//Police files of the world spurt out in a blast of bone meal//Street gangs Uranian born in the face of appalling conditions//Will Hollywood never learn? The Dummy Revolt flashed round the world when they took it to Cut City .. and talked out of turn and threw the WORDS AND IMAGE back//and dragged the down graders out of their cool blue houses and kicked the frozen flesh beings into screaming slate crystals on the street of brass and copper. Under the dead sun. Unimaginable and downright stupid Disaster/Teen age future time...
IF YOU CHARGE THE SOFT MACHINE DIRECTLY THE MACHINE DIRECTLY CHARGED BY YOUR HATE.
Attack machine directly:

MISTAKE OF LATE CAPTAIN AHAB.
Enemy advance we retreat/Cut word lines Minutes to Go/Enemy retreat we advance/free door ways/enemy encamp we agitate/shift linguals/enemy tire we attack/Rub out all the machine words forever. Rub out machine word THE forever. The sender of the soft machine?
"Meet your old top kick boys. May have given you a bad time. Write it all up to training."

"The SOFT MACHINE?: An obstacle course. Basic training for space. I quote: write the enemy into friends. Write the soft machine out in training. Write the enemy into space. The enemy only exist in word. In word THE. Rub out word THE forever. "I Uranian willy the heavy metal kid perfected the big con hey rube switch along the tang dynasty. I let them set up the big store /the prop banks/and float their counterfeit replica stock syn/thesized from cabbage and banker Droppings. Then I pull the switch and the stock is GOOD. The board is HONEST. The big store is free. The bank will redeem all promissory notes. Board syndicates and powers of the earth .. pay. Pay PAY. I have pulled the time switch and the time jerked positi on disin/tegrating virus from the first. Time was my plant. I have then pulled the big con hey rube switch. And luced my fatal light! The cool blue police of Uranian willy drift over the earth.
Checking board books police files of the world with fingers light and cold as Spring Wind. Checking the Thing Police/ checking the word and image bank and all the agenst of trak.

And America most heavily infected area on the Board /America was culture to grow resistant strains./"Sub virus stimulates anti-virus special group .. Argue second time a/round such a deal" minutes to go. "Not knowing what is and is not knowing I KNEW NOT."
--Hassan I Sabbah's Razor.

NOW THE AREA OF TOTAL PAIN TOTAL ALERT TOTAL WAR: Flash bulb of total urgency blezes in all out faces pass the mirror lines streets in neon swirls. Total competition for Space Prize. Move and Counter Move cancel OUT the board as chessmen go up in bit/ter almond vapor. Without love junk cover orgasm severs word lines leave agents no or/ders wherewith to merge one another into one character to bug almost every body as "Klinkers": Agents who operate outside the lines saying most awful things totally un-top secret to top annihilating all."

from: the emerald city

. . . for Gregory Corso

Oh ye dead who waken in the underground rooms
the loud fraud palaces of garnets and dreams, the dry water,
the cold fire
the small green emerald men, thick as green ants

Oh ye dead who waken in dead caverns
on the front porch, under the canvas
your nose striped like a barber's pole, and no way to explain it,
or in the back seat of a car,
clown-hatted at the marriage of one card to another,
the intercourse of Leopard spots,
shout white! what's all the use? black blood
growing on the ground, terror in the shape of water come.

And the water. Cold. Lifeless. Shake it! Look, it refuses
     to answer!
Oh water, why so soggy that you can't stand up straight?
Glazed by water, glass-eyed by garnets, creased by green men,
     what's the matter Nobody would let you in!

You, on the front porch.
You, in the back seat of the sedan.
Did you forget to use the door and flew in on a bat wing?
Magic makers, no wonder
they've still got you webbed in the hall. I know your feet get tired
     as spittoons.
I know your sleeves look sometimes like the butts of someone else's
     cigarette,
I know this vestibule
is your whole hotel, baggage! Your bridal suite of one thousand
     rooms.

rel bore speng lule

And you are damned out of hand—
mauve lipped you seek consolation
in the acorn's bitter core
masking against sanity or confession

Confusion swelling out of the ground
could never contain you
though you willed to be burned
tormenting the spell of witchery

The bitchery in which you are self enveloped
writhing eel purple and magic
in electrical plunging
                  hip leashed
the periphery cain babeling in treason
haunting reason against night call
of fornicating frogs, wart bloated

So you are damned
               the lip curl
fashioned in a debtor's hell
though your liniments are jewel brilliant
your tang rich and cool as honey

pastoral

The furrow, opening out, cool
warming in the sun
receiving seed, covered

Oh lovely body, yours

Tracy Thompson

stranger

A red tree   a bird or two
High sun and scarecrow in the cornfield
A man in a greyblue car passing
Thinking   if the birds were flying
If I were standing
             the sun is too bright
Is the bird singing?

Paul Carroll

what did
your face look like before
you were conceived by your
father & your mother?

—But
        why does this voice shock
me? As if a stranger
        with dark cold fingers,
suddenly, without a word,
        grazed your pubic hair:
                Caruso—
                your voice so lucid
                & remote
                over the FM

There is a part of me
that was
before my mother bore me—
                obscure & palpitating,
muscular, my own. Restless,

I fidget with the letters on my desk;
pay *Big Table's* trucking bill to Frisco;
try to concentrate on an article on Castro in *The Nation*

                (A yellow celluloid collar
                & prickly union suit
                looped about a rockingchair:
            this raw rank German odor in the air:
        I am my grandfather Grill's big freckled knuckles
        grappling pigiron by a Bessmer
        or stacking pinochle chips on Archer Avenue:
                scorch of syph)   All week

I've daydreamed that I caught a dose

                (Stiff
                brandnew derby
                cocked on the boy's red head:
            he squats in fresh mud milking
            the udders of a nanny goat

halfconcealed by an Irish fog)

Were you happy
when I circulated in your testicles?

> Who
> are we anyway?
> The clouds inside the heart
> ocean sun
> those silent & eternal birds

The doctor's prophylactic glove, probing,
while I hunch primitive, spread-
eagle, stiffarming
the office wall.   That
halfcrazed tough fantastic Bishop:

> "Do
> nothing
> to prevent my martyrdom:
> I hear the murmur of the living waters in me,
> saying:
> Go
> Ignatius
> to the Father"

> *Patrem*
> *veni Patrem veni*

Father: your semen burns my face

G. C. Oden

lay your head here

Lay your head here. Let the hollow of my
shoulder shelter as leaf-light on your forehead I touch down. Keep quiet now. Deep-breathe
it (like a well) while soft-safe in my arms
I marry you. Love in its steep is best,
uplifting through its salt of pooled despair;
and when, at highest providence, it proves
byways of blood tidelands of care. Now is
that time; now, as we total one we two
who, hanged by old griefs, drown now in this new.

James Boyer May

the salutary snare

. . . for Colin Wilson

Inveiglement's the word . . .
invokes the muttered-hoarsley animals
of darkly-omened paths
for looped and twisted snouts: waylaid,
coerced, onstumbling victims—headless,
jerked into iniquity.

HOW-WHEN-WHICH matters not; but heed
the 'free' beast's counter-tale
of satiation's aisles to boredom.
All aimless wanderers are chosen
for this easy-nibbled pasturage . . . greenly
everyway, through timeless foliage.

Indulgenced leap's discoveries:
how Eden's banishment purveyed
the apple-bane . . . unsimply-fevering
childhoods . . . luring all conditions . . .
never pleading tags for purpose . . . or, with
grownup buggeries as substitutes,
till bites won't lust on fairest-odored vines.
Instead, the grand maleficence,
which saves each beast despair . . . by
twisting tight the guide against omniscience.

Better than to dally, wondering
if somewhere sometime next to fall
on meaning-change, to compensate for straying . . .
safe-in-pain; to baleful self-betrayal.

Marc D. Schleifer

here & there . . . *for Marian's Show*

Here—
swirls, circles,
curvy scimitars,
the Crescent reappears.

A Berber in the marketplace   more red-faced Irish
than Frank O'Hara
so I guess it fits.

dolorous somewhere behind

dolorous somewhere behind
scotchwind massages leaves in
  many trees
nervously can
slightly by increasing for an
  instant
(held back watchful by moist
  salivasalt)
climax tear them from their
  holding
tantalizes sensuous
like the knowing expert fingers
  of a skillful
woman telling your body what
  she seeks
(give in for she has claws)

I too felt the diverse fingers of
  the wind
on the narrow beach as I
looked out to sea intent upon
  my
purpose waiting for the fires
  out there
yet in my inner ear I breathed
  still
waiting for the leaves to scream

I seek the fires rising from
the sea
(not Poseidon nor Odysseus
they are dead)

help me look for the fires
help me look for the fires

like the harlot for the sailors
expectant and anxious
(almost a welcomed dread that

here at last is what we
all have taken off our longjohns
  for)

like the priest for the vision
succumbent and submissive
(almost a religious vigil that
now with it in sight we all
can feel in it a warmth)

like the queer for the male
  bathers
breathless and passioned
(almost a maniacal perversion
  that
when we do see them we
feel our bowels tightentingleflow)

help me look for the fires
for I too like the others
for I too like the harlot
for I too like the priest
for I too like the queer
for I too wait keep watch all
  night
nodding between sleep and
  desire
expectancy and submission
and all the other feelings I have
  had
have now ever will have
(and more)

watch and wait for the fires
  that will
spring out from the sea
to match the power of the
  wind that
comes to goes from me

Gene Frumkin

the fat pigeon

Here we are, handcuffed to our bodies.
Everything that touches us
leaves a criminal in our blood.
My friend, we exist

under an impossible esthetic:
each sentiment of incense,
of plume and honeysuckle,
conceals a policeman;

even our skins are watching us.
We are Negro, friend, and the law is white.
We must love each other cruelly, as a vise,
fearing only the fat pigeon in the heart.

Jonathan Williams

the big house

. . . for Sherwood Anderson

plant
    candles about you,

dance nude thru Wisconsin, prance
                  to the factory,
feeling the cloven hoof root
             flowers
about the business shoe . . .

see no one, ever more,
makes mess upon thy temple floors

cast celebration,
      like a seed:

a mote—more,
        a pomegranate, a red
planet between the teeth
           (seeth thou both big and
little of it)

     spit it, far out

William Corrington

hard man

there was this somewhat man
whose rotten liver
stained his cheeks
dark tan
who approved
spiny marvels
the stench
of suddenness

the otherbody hurt of
quick withdrawal

who loved so bad so many
(once up on a time) til
a deft gash cut him down

and he dying awfully
called on tenderness

and spurted stone

Kay Boyle

print from a lucite block

Last night as I crossed
The black ice toward your image
A deer ran.

The fume of his breath fled
As he leapt sprang ran
Bearing the constellations
On his high branched head.

And my heart like the deer
Asked that carrot fern, turnips, fresh greens
Proffer their leaves despite the month
The time of year.

The words to say this hung, mute spears
That had been running water once and ceased.
In the night's black glass
Your image turned from shadow to moonlight
As the antlered deer leapt past.

Paul Blackburn

death watch : Veille d'Hiver

Intravenous is a lousy replacement
for a plate of baked ham and potatoes.

   With the mercury below O
you check the thermometer each time you leave the house
   and report the new figure back
   as tho it were vital statistic.
It is hard to know what is best.

So the man lies there in that white bed,
   groaning sometimes,
breathing loudly against his hour, restless
against his inaction, tossing
unconscious, but that is no rest.

   Luckily, the perfection
   of the unbroken shapes of the world
   under the new snowfall
   after the mercury rose,
   gives us no hope at all
   luckily for us.

Clayton Eshleman

red shoes .. from songs for exile

   Her fingers on my collar
         poinsettias in autumn
   crackling of reeds bent into baskets,
   O dry mouth of the lily . . .
        we walk through
   fingers tearing corn, four men joking,
   odor of bubbling pozole under a calve's head
   furry with flies . . .
       I would talk with you
   but your name is Spain
      your eyes lift
   towards Barcelona where your mother
   glides the dusktime patio
   birds
     in every hand . . .

great

Great day
Great day in the morning
Great Northern
Great anguish
Great compromise
Great rock of Gibralter
Great Carlsbad Caverns
Great Isosceles Triangle
Great horrible mummy
Great memory of the sacred dead
  (secret)
Great timetable
Great avalanche
Great maneuverability
Great jumping crawfish and
  Jehosophat
Great faker of us all
Great capitalist, immortal cellist
  of magnolia dreams:
  Andrew J. Mecklefus
Great Capricorn or cancer
Great calamity
Great golly
Great gee grim yesterdays!
Great gallomperin goloshes
Great sufferin sinnedfish
Great Caliope & Sweet Corn
  RailWay
Great pop tune & jackass stable
Great barnacles across America's
  crabless waterways
Great consternation among the
  countless constellations
Great cornhuskers of Nebraska,
  Wyoming and the North
  Central states
Great fartcatchers: Dizzy &
  Daffy Bean!
Great bombardiers
Great ladies, Methodist & Negro
  Sowthern & All-White
Great California melons!

Great husky hugs & dogs in the
  snow
Great carolinas, winds of the
  peconos
Great Samson—Morgue of the
  Amalekites
Great cod! (codpiece not
  included)
Great Crackers. Great bits of
  the South
Great New York. Paradise of
  pickle pushers
Great Constantinople formerly
  great Istanbul
Great Rome—glory of Pops
  Swing that chausible!
  Make it plausible
  It's so adorable.
  That Thomistian rag
Great cockroaches of Brooklyn
  & the South Bronx—I salute
  you
Great Whitman who now owns
  a publishing Co.
  & Jefferson a savings bank
  & Franklin a correspondence
  courser
Great tariffs. Protect american
  women
Great golfers protect american
  sures
Great U2 protect our protectors
  as we protect theirs
Great irony—these are stealy
  times
Great bagle—bakers—sowers of
  immortal circles
Great lox merchants—dealers
  in the bellies of others
Great Platonic apples falling
  on Newtonian heads
  Von Braun caws:

*Shall their rockets excede that
  of Urs?*
Great unnecessaries blossoming
  in our butcher shops, our
  corner drug stories
  Is this zipper necessary?
Great jobs to tame or tease the
  multiprudes:
    Five weeks in Hawaii with
      back pay for lifers
Great machines—artificial
  nipples
    Laws for everyone!
Great skyrockets—"Plead
  Guilty!"
Great Evangels: Your death is
  coming!
Great song at midnight
    Sing!
    The roof is falling
& man WHEN THE ROOF
  FALLS
Look . . .
    The great sky

Barbara Moraff

a little spur

Since you cut out baby of my
  flesh a
Funny whistle scratching dawn
  on the
Nape of my neck hot like an
  old hag going young
Again
Since you cut out baby of my
  flesh a
thistlewierd hum copping my
  twisted
bloody gut & belly
      bold
          So let the gods
            spring forth idiots
          my sun is shining
Tho it's a little
              in drag

Sam Abrams

bodies only

d'ya really think I'm a fool
to work at tryn to knock off
a piece like you?

& what about the hollyhocks
& the sun eh?

as if you're bugged, being
what every man (give me credit)
desires.

formal re:

I sing my baby to sleep
with your songs you
son of a bitch

& hum your songs
on the beach in the sun

you work at bastarding &
met me with hate
long time ago

in small worlds from
here to me & you
of all trying

you forgot to touch 2nd!

sucker I sing my baby to sleep
with your songs

Terence McGuire

mid-morning

Either a baby is crying
Or a machine sighing
But it's a bitch nevertheless
When one is thirty years old
  and unpublished
Playing Joe Smiley in an
  upstairs back office
    Over city hall.

88

NEW DEPARTURES

international review of literature & the lively arts

new departures in

prose

from: paul ableman samuel beckett william s burroughs michael hamburger raymond queneau alan sillitoe

in poetry

from: kenneth beaudoin robert beloof patrick bowles pete brown alan brownjohn gregory corso robert creeley donald davie allen ginsberg john fuller charles hamblett anselm hollo michael horovitz hans helms piero heliczer dennis keene bernard kops jack kerouac adrian mitchell john miles mike mcclure om gabriel pearson raymond queneau jon silkin august stramm charles tomlinson sir herbert read philip o'connor judy spink stevie smith

plays

from: samuel beckett dick higgins eugene ionesco john mcgrath harold pinter stefan themerson

painting

from: alberto burri alan davie anthony hill anna lovell victor pasmore franciszka themerson bob rauschenberg kurt schwitters picasso

music

from: john cage cornelius cardew earl brown charlie mingus lamonte young

and multifarious photo collage images of wonder fifteen issues in preparation advance $15 or singles at $1.50 post free from 57 Greek Street, London W 1

Pub. Sq. (*Continued from p. 4*)

"Hear? I hear the pigeons."

"Say," I said, "you can't hear pigeons in this bombardment."

The old man smiled.

"Listen, you can't hear birds down here." I looked up. The pigeons were gone.

"Do you hear them now?"

"Yes," he said.

"Listen, man," I said. I looked about me. Across the Square the pigeons were eating breadcrumbs near the waterpond. I listened. I heard streetcars clattering past, automobile horns, shuffling feet. I heard a distant foghorn.

"Listen, man. You—you—"

"Khrushchev, Khrushchev—"

A fat man stopped. "Press?"

He took the paper and turned to the financial page. He stood there reading.

A woman stopped. She was small and plainly dressed, but very sweet-looking. She looked about 35. "P. D.," she said.

I stood looking at the pigeons.

"How are you tonight?" asked the woman.

"Very well, thank you," said the blind man.

I looked up at the Terminal Tower.

"Many sales today?" said the woman.

"Oh, so many, so many."

The pigeons passed my view of the Tower. They must have risen of a sudden.

A streetcar stopped. Three small children stepped off.

I said offstage to the woman, "He tells me he can hear the pigeons."

She smiled. "Two of them are his. He used to have flocks of them. They're all dead but two. When one dies he tells me." She smiled sweetly. "He always knows when one dies."

"But how can he?" I asked.

"Oh, he knows."

"But how?"

"He tells me. I've known him for years. He knows lots that we don't know. He's not so blind."

"You mean—"

"No, I don't mean he's faking. He's blind all right."

The fat man grunted and I looked at him. He was chewing his cigar angrily. "Damned idiots!" he said. He said it to the paper.

The three small children were standing in the Square staring up at the Civil War monument.

A pretty girl passed.

"Listen," I said, "how can he hear birds in this bombardment?"

"Khrushchev—Press, P. D.—"

"Damned idiots," said the fat man again.

"His ears," said the woman. "They're sensitive to them."

The fat man folded his paper abruptly.

The three small children turned and crossed the street toward the Terminal Tower.

The pigeons were eating again.

"My ears are sensitive to them," said the blind man.

An intersection cop blew his whistle.

The fat man looked at us. There was a funny look on his face. All the color had gone out of his cheeks. "I used to raise pigeons," he said.

(*Continued on page 100*)

Walter Lowenfels
FOTO: JERRY STOLL

Ray Bremser Allen Ginsberg

FRANK BALANTRIE

Leslie Woelf Hadley

Curtis Zahn

ANGE

WILLIAM BURROUGHS

FOTO: BRION GYSIN

clayton eshleman

Robert Sward
FOTO: B. B. PERRY

Margaret Randall

TERENCE McGUIRE

Ann Giudici

Sorrentino

Paul Blackburn

GENE FRUMKIN

Mike McClure

JUDSON CREWS

Jon Edgar Webb, Jr.

Gary Snyder

CONTRIBUTORS

RUSSELL EDSON writes: "I've just brought out a book APPEARANCES, Fables & Drawings on a handpress, handset, 17 drawings, and in 1961 Jonathan Williams' Jergon Books will bring out WHAT A MAN CAN SEE & OTHER FABLES by me, drawings by Ray Johnson."

SINCLAIR BEILES lives in Paris, from where he manipulates indefatigable contact with most of the Continent's validly creative experimental writers & poets. In 1960 he wrote MINUTES TO GO with William Burroughs, Brion Gysin & Gregory Corso. His recent EXPLOSION APARTHEID in the International Literary Annual published by John Calder, in which Burroughs, Gysin and Stuart Gordon also appear, helped put him into the spotlight along with them under the label: The New Exiles. He is currently engaged in preparing a programme of simple narrative poems for the BBC.

STUART GORDON whom Beiles calls a "non-gravitational dramatist" recently deserted Paris and is now somewhere in New York City.

GREGORY CORSO, who wrote GASOLINE and THE HAPPY BIRTHDAY OF DEATH and many other commoving works, including BOMB, is back in Paris from Germany and Greece to imbibe to his latest book THE AMERICAN EXPRESS published by Olympia Press.

JON EDGAR WEBB, JR. lives in California. He is the son of the Editor of OUTSIDER, and his prose piece in this issue is an excerpt from a novel in progress. He is also an artist.

ANN GIUDICI, formerly a dancer with Martha Graham, is now Public Relations Director for the East Side House Settlement in NYC. She has a one-act off-Broadway play now under consideration; this is her first publication with poetry. She is the mother of twin boys.

DIANE DI PRIMA is co-editor with LeRoi Jones of THE FLOATING BEAR, 309 E. Houston St., NYC. Her distinctive small volume of poems THIS KIND OF BIRD FLIES BACKWARD (Totem Press) was an immediate sellout. Walter Lowenfels says of her: "She is one of the best since Sappho." A Swarthmore girl, she can talk Beat idiom as if she invented it.

JOHN GRANT of Edinburgh, Scotland, is 26. He studied music in Glasgow, but resigned in his final year for a career in films; is currently engaged as assistant to Forsyth Hardy, Director of Films of Scotland, and has scripted a number of documentary films including "A Song for Prince Charlie." His story in this issue appeared also in SIDEWALK, the Edinburgh literary "little" so ably edited by Alex Neish which recently folded because of "out of cash."

PAUL HAINES after finishing school (AB Psychology) went to Paris, then into 2 years at the University of Grenoble, then to Turkey and other places, and is now back in NYC, writing.

GARY SNYDER is 31, a graduate of Reed College where he majored in mythology. He studied linguistics at Indiana University and classical Chinese at Berkeley. He lives in Japan, where he went in 1956 to study formal Zen training. His books RIPRAP (Origin Press), & MYTHS AND TEXTS (Totem/Corinth) have been received with critical acclaim.

GAEL TURNBULL, until recently editor of the much-liked MIGRANT, was born in Edinburgh and educated at Cambridge and in Canada and the U. S. He is now a medical doctor in Ventura, California, but finds time to write and is widely-published in poetry and critical essays. Origin Press pub. his volume BJARNI.

CHARLES OLSON was born in 1910 and lives in Gloucester, Mass. He has taught at Clark, Harvard and Black Mountain College, where he was instructor and rector, 1951-56. Among his many books are CALL ME ISHMAEL (Reynal, Hitchcock), THE MAXIMUS POEMS (Jargon), and NEW MAXIMUS POEMS (Jargon/Corinth).

EDWARD DORN is 32; was educated at the University of Illinois and Black Mountain College. He lives in Santa Fe, N.M. Much-published, his work was reprinted in THE NEW AMERICAN POETRY 1945-60. One of his best-known critical efforts is his WHAT I SEE IN THE MAXIMUS POEMS (Migrant). A must for Olson devotees.

ALLEN GINSBERG's most recent book is KADDISH: POEMS 1957-60 (City Lights, 1961), which beat us to publication with his poem in this issue. His famous (academic critics say "infamous") HOWL will presently hit the 100,000-sales mark. He is perhaps the most controversial poet on the literary pro-&-con scene since Walt Whitman. He has read to multitudes of university students. An adoptee of the Beat Generation, he succumbed awhile to its Call of the Wild; is now reemerging along evident indications of stricter discipline and a steadily maturing perspective; viz: the gas is turned down but the pot is still boiling.

PETER ORLOVSKY is 28; lives with Allen Ginsburg in NYC, or in London or Paris. His first publication was in Yugen; later in THE BEAT SCENE, and NEW AMERICAN POETRY 1945-60.

LANGSTON HUGHES, whose many commendable works are post-era protest literature (today with surface & token integration in many areas the protest element in Negro writing is being replaced by surer "equality" efforts), was educated at Columbia and Lincoln Universities. While at Lincoln he won the Witter Bynner Prize for undergraduate poetry and wrote his novel NOT WITHOUT LAUGHTER. He went on to publish numerous plays and poems, and in 1931 he won the Harmon Award and in 1935 a Guggenheim Fellowship.

JUAN MARTINEZ is 19, lives in Seattle, and has a one-man show of his paintings about to materialize. He has written some poetry and a novel, but his story in this issue is his first published piece of writing.

GILBERT SORRENTINO was educated at Brooklyn College and served in the Army 1951-53. He was the editor of NEON, a highly-rated "little" magazine which he suspended in 1959. A volume of his poems THE DARKNESS AROUND US was published by Jargon/Corinth in 1960. Grove reprinted him in NEW AMERICAN POETRY 1945-60.

WALTER LOWENFELS, one of our guiding lights in preparing OUTSIDER 1, is the author of seven books of poetry & criticism; he compiled and edited WALT WHITMAN'S CIVIL WAR (Knopf, 1960), and lives in Mays Landing, N.J., with his wife, Lillian, who also is a poet & well-known translator. In 1930 Lowenfels shared with E. E. Cummings the Richard Aldington Award and in 1959 the Longview Foundation Award. His two poems in this issue are part of a work titled SURVIVAL which appeared in the Feb. 1960 issue of Mainstream. WALT WHITMAN'S CIVIL WAR was a Book-of-the-Month June dividend. The Outsider urges its readers to buy a copy - or to beg, borrow or purloin one - at the earliest opportunity.

CID CORMAN, the editor of ORIGIN, writes us that the magazine will be reissued for another 5 years, beginning sometime during 1961.

LAWRENCE FERLINGHETTI's poem in this issue is slated to be included in his forthcoming book of poems entitled STARTING FROM SAN FRANCISCO to be published this year by New Directions. The poem was written in the course of a sleepless night while guesting with us last December, and after an evening of talk with kaja.

MARGARET RANDALL, our N. Y. area Editor, is the author of two volumes of poetry: GIANT OF TEARS and ECSTASY IS A NUMBER. Her poems have appeared in Liberation, Nomad, Provincetown Review, White Dove Review & others. She is the mother of a very young son, Gregory,

Turn to page 94

despite which she has been, and still is, of immense help to us with our OUTSIDER chores.

MILLEN BRAND whom we met in '36 in a soda parlor in Greenwich Village & haven't seen since is now in Monte Carlo, Monaco, working on his book LOCAL LIVES from which his poem in this issue is taken. Among other achievements, he authored THE OUTWARD ROOM, & is a grandfather.

ROBERT CREELEY who edited the famed BLACK MOUNTAIN REVIEW with a Harvard background is now teaching in Guatemala. He is the author of 7 books, among them A FORM OF WOMEN (Jargon/ Corinth) and SHORT STORY III (Scribner's). In 1960 he received the D. H. Lawrence Fellowship.

MIKE MCCLURE, 29, has pub. much poetry. Among his volumes of poems are PASSAGE (Jargon,1956) FOR ARTAUD (Totem, 1959), HYMNS TO ST. GERYON & OTHER POEMS (Auerhahn, 1959); and Grove is bringing out soon THE NEW BOOK/A BOOK OF TORTURE. He lives & writes in San Francisco.

CHARLES BUKOWSKI, 40, is a prolific & ever-maturing poet whose work has appeared in more than half a hundred literary magazines, netting him less than enough $ to spend an evening on the Strip in Los Angeles, where he lives in as much isolation as locked doors & drawn shades in a big city permits. Last year Hearse Press brought out his first book of poems FLOWER, FIST AND BESTIAL WAIL. 7 Poets Press has another in preparation - and if we manage to acquire a motorized printing press to replace the handpress we've got now we hope to pub. him as No. 1 in our planned GYPSY LOU SERIES of poetry & prose chapbooks.

ROBERT SWARD, 28, has a B.A. from the U. of Illinois, and an M.A. from the U. of Iowa. He is much-published, and is currently studying on a Fullbright grant in England.

HARLAND RISTAU's poems have been appearing in the "littles" for a decade. 7 Poets Press issued a collection of his work this year under the title: NEXT TIME YOU'RE ALIVE.

COLIN WILSON is both the praised and abused author of the controversial book THE OUTSIDER (Houghton Mifflin) - after which we did not name this magazine. The idea for our OUTSIDER was born about the same time Wilson was.

JORY SHERMAN, our West Coast Editor, is 27; a ex-adv. man turned poet. Must be a diplomat too, for he's ironed out a lot of woe for us in the West. He's appeared in many "littles" and has one volume of poems published, SO MANY ROOMS (Galley Sail), and another forthcoming.

LESLIE WOOLF HEDLEY was educated at NYU and at Oxford U. in England. In 1949 he founded INFERNO PRESS EDITIONS, and says it is "the only independent press still publishing in San Francisco." He has appeared in Prairie Schooner, Literary Review, Meanjin, Mutiny, Colorado Review, many others; and has been translated into German, Japanese, French & Yiddish. Was in the U.S. Army 1942 to 1946.

HENRY MILLER has moved back overseas. Grove Press meanwhile is publishing his long forbidden book TROPIC OF CANCER, on June 24, 1961.

LEROI JONES is the well-known poet publisher of Totem Press, and the editor of YUGEN.

MARVIN BELL, our Midwest Editor, has been pub. in more than two-score of the "littles" and is the Editor of statements. He also is a creative photographer, a creative critic, and has been of vast creative help to us in many ways.

LESTER EPSTEIN is an artist too, with many exhibitions in Mexico & in Europe. He was educated at Wash. U. & The Royal College of Art (London). A book of his poems MIRACLE AND TREADMILL was pub. in Mexico in 1957; he has six more in preparation. Now in New Orleans.

CURTIS ZAHN whose work has been pub. in virtually all of the independent "littles" is director of The Pacificus Foundation, a non-

profit corp. sponsoring production of drama, literature, music, dance, the graphic arts,etc.

NOTE that space is running short so will have to start packing words closer and briefer.

WILLIAM BURROUGHS wrote last from Tangiers. He is the author of NAKED LUNCH, sections of which have appeared in Big Table, Black Mt. Review & Evergreen. Olympia Press pub. the book in France; it won't see pub. in U. S. for a long time to come. . . . kaja is a New Orleans poet of steadily growing stature, with filecases packed with poems that have never been sent out. Editors, take note. . . . JUDSON CREWS has been pub. repeatedly for years in many of the little magazines, and will continue to be. . . . TRACY THOMPSON lives in S.F.; he's appeared in a score of poetry journals. . . . . PAUL CARROLL is the editor of BIG TABLE. . . . G. C. ODEN has held creative writing awards from the John Hay Whitney Foundation, Yaddo, & is being pub. with increasing frequency in the important "littles". . . . JAMES BOYER MAY is the brave and hard-working editor of TRACE. . MARC D. SCHLEIFER is the editor KULCHUR, a little magazine of rising importance out of NYC. . . . FREDERICK PFISTERER III is 26; he grad. from Rutgers with a BA in English Lit. Is specializing in dramatic writing now in NYC. This is his first poetry publication. . . . GENE FRUMKIN is the capable editor of the dependable West Coast magazine COASTLINES. . . . JONATHAN WILLIAMS is the publisher of Jargon Books, Highlands, S. C. He has probably lost more money doing more good for writers deserving publication in book form than any other independent publisher we've ever known. . . . WILLIAM CORRINGTON is in the English Dept. at Louisiana State U. His work has appeared in Mutiny, San Francisco Review, Janus, Fiddlehead, Dalhousie Review, Olivant, Quagga, Sparrow, New Idea, Inland, Galley Sail Review, Claremont Quarterly, Patterns, others. . . . KAY BOYLE is the author of more than 20 volumes of short stories as well as 13 novels. She has received several O. Henry Memorial Prize awards for the Best Short Story of the Year. Of late her creative efforts have been leaning more toward poetry than ever before. . . . PAUL BLACKBURN attended NYU & the U. of Wisconsin. Got a BA from Wisconsin, was a Fullbright scholar, U. of Toulouse 1954-55. More study there, and then to Spain. His poems have been pub. in many of the "littles" - and in The New American Poetry 1945-60. He is also a translator & editor. . . . CLAYTON ESHLEMAN is beginning to receive his due in recognition, as evidenced by an increasing number of acceptances from editors of the more important "littles". He's been in Big Table, Coastlines, San Francisco Review, Trobar, Quixote, Inland, etc., His SONGS FOR EXILE, from which his poem in this issue is taken, is a book of poems set in a Mexican landscape which is close to completion. . . . TULI KUPFERBERG is the extremely sharp-witted editor of BIRTH coming out of NYC. . . . SAM ABRAMS who lived in Brooklyn 1935-58 is now in Urbana, Ill., with his wife and son, studying & teaching Greek and Latin. . . BARBARA MORAFF first appeared in Yugen. She was in THE BEAT SCENE and BEATITUDE ANTHOLOGY, and lives in NYC. . . . TERENCE MCGUIRE lives in Washington, D. C.; has read his poetry in coffee houses, but this is his first publication. . . . RAY BREMSER is 27, lived in Jersey City until recently; now somewhere South America. He is a graduate of Bordentown Ref. and has read his poetry at Vassar, Princeton, Lehigh, etc., in the company of Ginsberg, Jones, Corso and Orlovsky. Is married to Brenda; they have one or two children (we've lost his bio notes). He was included in THE NEW AMERICAN POETRY 1945-60, The Beat Scene, and has been much published in the "littles". MELVILLE HARDIMENT is our Editor in London & is a writer in close touch with the creative set in England. His wife, HARRIET CROWDER, a photographer on the magazine Design, took the pix on back cover of Beiles, Corso & Melville, and the one of Wm. Burroughs on page 75. Other Back Cover foto credits go to Cedric Wright for Henry Miller; Arthur Avedon for G.C.Oden; Arthur Siegel for Paul Carroll; Jerry Stoll for pix of Lillian and Walter Lowenfels.

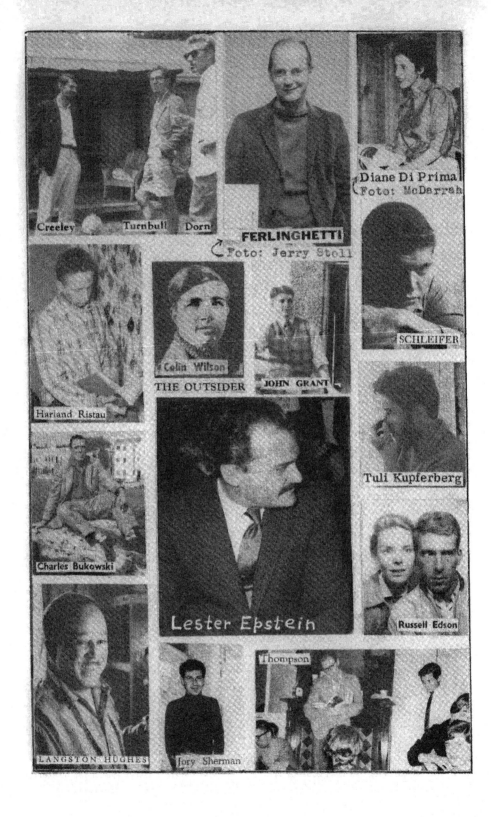

Creeley   Turnbull   Dorn

Diane Di Prima
Foto: McDarrah

FERLINGHETTI
Foto: Jerry Stoll

Colin Wilson
THE OUTSIDER

JOHN GRANT

SCHLEIFER

Harland Ristau

Tuli Kupferberg

Charles Bukowski

Lester Epstein

Russell Edson

Thompson

LANGSTON HUGHES   Jory Sherman

statements 4

~~~~~~

There's never been any publication quite like it!

Between Worlds

An International Magazine of Creativity Devoted entirely to the Creative Imagination. No criticism, no book reviews, no politics. Fresh new writers and original work by the most famous writers of the world. Mainly in English, but also in Spanish, Italian, Portuguese, French and German. Movements from Dadaism to Beatism represented.

"Much straight thinking must have gone into it. Congratulations!
—William Carlos Williams

"A great success, in its total effect much beyond my expectations. Verse selections strikingly good."
—George Dillon

" . . . your splendid magazine which has interested me so much and which I am so delighted to possess."
—John Cowper Powys

"Between Worlds . . . seems a very good job to me."
—Lawrence Durrell

"Can be recommended to all college and larger public libraries."
—Library Journal

Published twice a year, spring and fall
For a one-year subscription send $2 to

Between Worlds
Inter American University
San Germán, Puerto Rico

◆◇◆

now available

KULCHUR 3

William S. Burroughs	Jack Kerouac
Paul Bowles	Allen Ginsberg
Paul Goodman	Gregory Corso
Charles Olson	Diane Di Prima
LeRoi Jones	Gary Snyder
Joel Oppenheimer	Gilbert Sorrentino

others

$1.00   Subscription $4.00

KULCHUR
888 Park Ave., NY 21, NY

A limited number of copies of **KULCHUR's** 1 & 2
are still available for $1.00

NOMAD

Box 626
Culver City, California
Editors: Donald Factor
          Anthony Linick

Featuring;

The New American Poetry,
1961 thru Infinity.

Materials from the European
avant garde; selected, edited,
and translated by our European
Correspondent: Anselm Hollo.

"The Sullen Art," interviews
with the literary creators of
tomorrow, supervised and
designed by David Ossman, the
originator of this WBAI, New
York, feature.

An enlarged format designed to
bring to our readers a greater
selection of the best of contemporary poetry, fiction, criticism,
art work.

In Number Nine, the work of
Allen Ginsberg, Denise
Levertov, Le Roi Jones, Lew
Welch, and plenty of people
you've never heard of.

A One year's sub: $3.00
Single Issues: .75
The Complete Back File: $6.00

AGENDA

Volume 2, Nos. 2 & 3
(January 1961) contains
JEAN COCTEAU'S great
poem LEOUN
translated by ALAN NEAME

Cover designed by
Jean Cocteau.

Copies available from the
editor, William Cookson

New College, Oxford, England
35 cents each. Subscription
(12 issues) $2.

outburst

malcolm, logue, combs,
snyder, turnbull, dawson,
dorn, horovitz, creeley,
fletcher, hollo, heliczer,
black, brown for No.1. out
end april/beginning of may.
And for No. 2 (if enough
space) ginsberg, mcclure,
maclise, heliczer, jones,
rumaker, woolf, eigner,
meltzer, ball. subs 10/-or
$2.50 a year. basement, 167
amhurst rd. london e8.

YUGEN 7   Stops collections. De-camp. To wider
disposals. Registrations. Come to this, friends!
Discursiveness, till now frowned on, for this shot, &
later, a definite feature. Essays, or critical pieces.
Creeley's, Sorrentino's, Jones's. Also letters abt those
registrations. The 64 dollar question. Where are you, now
that, &c. These by Oppenheimer, Eigner, O'Hara. Also
some poems by George Stanley, Bruce Boyd, Gregory
Corso, Stuart Perkoff, Philip Whalen, Max Finstein, John
Ashberry, Mike McClure. Olson has prose & Koch a
play. All these are interesting decisions. To be so,
attractive. Now.

Two Cities

*The Bilingual Review
from Paris*

37 rue de la Bucherie, Paris 5

Editor, Jean Fanchette

Has published the most disturbing authors of France, England and America during its first year of publication.

Next issues will carry contributions by: William Burroughs, Michel Butor, Sinclair Beiles, Henry Miller, Lawrence Durrell, Beckett, Thirlwall, Yves Bonnefoy, John Ashbery, Jean Fanchette, Daisy Aldan, Kenward Elmslie, Jacques Dupin, many others—and a Portfolio on American Abstract Painters in Paris.

Subscription: $3 a year to: Daisy Aldan, 325 E. 57th St. New York City 28, N. Y.

SATIS

a little magazine: edited by Matthew Mead and published by Malcolm Rutherford.

Number Two contained spring 1961 Poems by Anne Cluysenaar, Bernice Ames, anselm hollo, Barriss Mills and Richard Weber. 'A Gesture to be clean'—Gael Turnbull on William Carlos Williams.

Number Three summer 1961: "Poems from America"—by Frederick Eckman, Larry Eigner, Charles Edward Eaton, Kent Gardien, Godfrey John, Robert Sward, Gael Turnbull, David Rafael Wang and others. 'The American dollar: a contemplation'—an unwritten study by the publisher.

40 cents ($1.20 for three issues) from: 21 Lyndhurst Avenue, Newcastle upon Tyne 2., England.

NOW AVAILABLE:

"*What I See in the Maximus Poems*" (Prose) by Edward Dorn; and "*A Poem in nine Parts*" by Matthew Mead, at 2/- or .35 each.

"*The Dancers Inherit the Party*", Selected Poems by the young Scottish poet Ian Hamilton Finlay, at 3/6 or .50.

"*The Whip*", Selected Poems by Robert Creeley, at $1 or 6/-. (Hard Cover edition 9/ or $2.)

"*Sovpoems*", Translations & introduction by Edwin Morgan. 32 pages, type-litho text, at 3/6 or .65.

"*Texts & Finnpoems*", Original poems in English and translations from his native Finnish, by Anselm Hollo. 28 pages, card cover, at 3/6 or .50.

Due Summer, 1961: "*It Seems It Was Persephone*", a poem sequence by Michael Shayer, at 2/- or .35.

Some copies of the last double issue of **MIGRANT**, including work by Morgan, Olson, Shayer, Mills, Dudek, Duncan, Bonheim, Fisher and others, at 2/- or .35.

All from: **MIGRANT**, 1199 Church St., Ventura, Calif. or 2 Camp Hill Road, Worcester, England.

BIG TABLE

1316 N. Dearborn   Chicago 10, Illinois

Fiction Poems Essays Art

4

THE NEW POETS

poems: ASHBURY
BLACKBURN
CORSO
CREELEY
FERLINGHETTI
GINSBERG
LOGAN
O'HARA
& OTHERS

art: FRANZ KLINE

essays: Creeley: SOME ORTS FOR THE SPORTS
Ginsberg: NOTES ON YOUNG POETS
Carroll: FIVE POETS IN THEIR SKINS

1

Kerouac
Corso*
Burroughs*

*1959 Longview Literary Awards

2

Dahlberg*
Bowles
Ginsberg

art: Leon Golub

3

Rechy
Genet
Mailer

art: Aaron Siskind

$1 per issue — $4 Vol. 1 No. 1 thru 4 — $7 Vol. 1 & 2

Pub. Sq. (*Continued from p. 90*)

"I can hear them talk," said the blind man.

"He always knows when one dies," said the woman.

I stood in the center of Cleveland and listened to people talk about pigeons. I was out of prison only a few hours. For years I'd been staring through prison bars. I'd stood in the prison yard watching the sky. I'd seen birds flying over the walls.

Once I found one of them lying in the prison hospital garden with a broken wing.

"Poor bird," I said.

I tried to fix the wing.

"What this wing needs," I said, "is nothing to do for awhile."

So I took the bird up to my cell on the fifth tier.

I fed it some crumbs.

When it died I dropped it in the rubbish box outside the west block door.

I thought, "Why don't I die? My wing is broken."

"Khrushchev—Press, P. D.—"

"Well, I must be going," said the woman.

I saw it was 5 o'clock.

"Come back," said the blind man.

"These pigeons don't get the the proper food," said the fat man.

"You look pale," I said to him.

"I feel pale," he said.

"Goodby," said the woman to all of us, smiling sweetly.

"One moment," I said. "You work?"

She looked at me in surprise.

"Certainly."

"It's nice to work." I didn't know what else to say.

"Nice to have work," she said, frowning. "But to work—" She smiled.

"Well, anyway, now you go home to rest."

"Now I go to work."

She glanced over her shoulder at the big Terminal Tower. "I help clean the inside of that thing," she said.

The three small children were standing near the entrance looking up.

"Goodby," said the woman.

"Goodby," I said.

"Pigeons are like babies," said the fat man.

Suddenly I asked, "What do you do?"

"Well," he said, "you can't just come right out and give a detailed account of how to raise them. You have—"

"I mean," I said, "what work are you in?"

"Oh, me." He shifted his cigar, and then clamped down on it. "I'm a gambler."

I nodded.

"This war—" he said. "You know we're at war right now, don't you?"

"Cold war?"

"War! And more casualties on their feet, with the dollar sinking, than in any arms war in history. And these now die slow."

"That why you're pale?" I had to say.

"Oh, I'm feeling better now."

"Kennedy, Kennedy. Press—"

I looked down. "You've been saying Khrushchev."

"Either one, they're both good for business."

"How about Castro?"

"Fair, fair," said the blind man.

"Wait'll he loses out," said the fat man. "Then watch the papers sell."

"Think he'll lose out?" I said.

"Damn right he will."

"There'll always be Castros, though. If this one loses out they'll soon make another one."

"Who will—the Communists?"

"The newspapers."

"Who are you?" he asked.

"I used to be a newspaperman."

"Well," said the fat man, "I used to own a newspaper."

"Khrushchev, Kennedy—"

I winked at the fat man. "He thinks he can hear those pigeons talking."

"Poor fellow," said the fat man softly.

The three small children were gone. A rush of traffic shot by. The pigeons were flying again. They flew up, up. They settled on the roof-edge of one of the small buildings at the west end of the Square.

The fat man went away saying, "See you again sometime."

I said, "Goodby, Mister," to the blind man.

This was in Cleveland a few hours after I was turned out of prison.

My wings felt no different.

CPSIA information can be obtained
at www.ICGtesting.com
Printed in the USA
BVOW06s0913181017
497997BV00021B/393/P